THE **ICE CREAM MAKER**
COMPANION

100 Easy-to-Make Frozen Desserts of All Kinds

Published by Gramercy Books, an imprint of Random House Value Publishing,
a division of Random House, Inc., New York.

Gramercy is a registered trademark and the colophon is
a trademark of Random House, Inc.

Random House
New York • Toronto • London • Sydney • Auckland
www.randomhouse.com

Edited by Shoshana Brickman

Printed and bound in China

Interior design by Ariane Rybski

A catalog record for this title is available from the Library of Congress.

ISBN 0-517-22746-0

10 9 8 7 6 5 4 3 2 1

THE **ICE CREAM MAKER**
COMPANION

100 Easy-to-Make Frozen Desserts of All Kinds

AVNER LASKIN

photography by DANYA

GRAMERCY BOOKS
New York

Table of Contents

ICE CREAM

I don't know anyone who doesn't like ice cream.

There are those who like to eat it on hot summer days, and others who indulge all year long. Some people prefer it creamy and smooth; others love finding chunks of nuts, chocolate, and fruit. Some people like it soft and light; others prefer it hard and dense, scooped with a glistening silver scoop. And that's not even mentioning all the tasty treats that can be created with ice cream—scooped on cones and in cups, layered in cakes and waffle sandwiches, mixed into sundaes and sodas. The list is as long as your imagination!

Making ice cream at home is a marvelous, almost magical experience. You simply take ordinary ingredients, mix them in the right proportions, heat them, chill them, then place them in an ice cream maker. You'll need a little patience, it's true, but the result is definitely worth it.

Also, when you make ice cream at home, you know exactly what goes into it. You can adjust the ingredients to suit special dietary needs, preferences, or occasions. You can make it as sweet and as rich as you want. You can even make it hot and spicy (see chili recipes) if you like! Homemade ice cream can be creamy or low-fat, hard or soft, smooth or textured, alcoholic, fruity, chocolaty, or nutty—you're making the ice cream, and you get to decide.

Preparing ice cream at home is also a great activity to do with children— they'll love adding their favorite ingredients, and have a great time enjoying the fruits of their efforts.

To begin with, learn the basic recipes, and become familiar with your ice cream maker. Every machine is a little different, and it may take a few tries until you learn how long it takes to reach the consistency you prefer. After you have mastered the basics, and taking into account the general rules below, you can adjust, alter, add, and experiment. Your enjoyment—and the enjoyment of everyone who is lucky enough to enjoy your ice cream—will be guaranteed.

Avner Laskin

Tips and Techniques

- Always use the freshest and highest quality ingredients for preparing your ice cream. Use fresh milk and fresh, large eggs. If your recipe calls for fruit, make sure it is ripe, but not overripe.

- Recipes that call for whole milk require milk that has a fat content of at least 3%.

- When a recipe calls for bittersweet chocolate, use high quality chocolate with at least 60% cocoa.

- When a recipe calls for coffee or espresso, you can use either instant or brewed. Just remember that the quality of the ice cream depends upon the quality of its ingredients—the better the coffee, the tastier the ice cream.

- Disinfect your ice cream maker according to the manufacturer's instructions after every use.

- *Custard* is the term used to describe the cooked mixture that goes into egg-based ice cream. The main ingredients in custard are cream, sugar, eggs, and flavoring.

- When cooking custard, use a candy thermometer to check the temperature. If the temperature is too high or too low, it will have a negative effect on the taste of the ice cream.

- After the custard has cooked, it must chill before going into the ice cream maker. Custard must be cooled for *at least* four hours in the refrigerator before placing in your ice cream maker. If possible, prepare the custard a day in advance, and store it in the refrigerator overnight.

- When pouring custard into the bowl of your ice cream maker, ensure the bowl is only 1/2 to 2/3 full. This gives the ice cream room to expand as it freezes.

- The texture of your ice cream is determined by how long the custard is in the ice cream maker. The principle is, the longer the custard is mixed in the ice cream maker, the harder and denser the ice cream. However, the actual time it takes to make an ice cream hard varies from one machine to the next. Get to know your ice cream maker, and your ice cream will soon come out exactly as you like.

- When first starting out, I recommend tasting the ice cream while it is in the ice cream maker (most people are pleased to do this) to test for consistency and lightness.

- When making chocolate ice cream, it is important to mix the chocolate into the warm custard while the chocolate is still totally melted. If the chocolate has cooled too much before you add it to the custard, the ice cream you produce will be grainy rather than smooth.

- In recipes that use alcohol, mix in the alcohol while the custard is still warm, so that the taste of the alcohol is fully incorporated into the custard.

- You can reduce or increase the amount of alcohol in a recipe, according to your preference. You can also omit alcohol from a recipe, if you like.

- Liquid ingredients can be substituted, as long as the total quantity of liquid in the recipe stays the same. For example, you can double the amount of whipping cream in a recipe and eliminate the whole milk, or vice versa. You can also substitute yogurt for whole milk or whipping cream, just make sure you use liquid yogurt, the kind meant for drinking, and not firm yogurt, the kind eaten with a spoon. Also, make sure the yogurt has a high enough fat content to give the ice cream the right creamy texture.

- You can use soya, rice, or coconut milk as a liquid substitute for cream or milk, just be sure to take into account whether the milk alternative you choose is sweetened. If so, alter the amount of sugar in the recipe accordingly.

- Some milk substitutes have a strong aftertaste, so make sure you like the milk substitute you are using before adding it to your ice cream.

- There are many types of vanilla flavoring, including whole beans, powder, and liquid extract. The best vanilla for making ice cream is vanilla bean, but if you can't find any in your grocery store, use the highest quality alternative.

- Although the recipes call for white sugar, you can substitute brown sugar as well. You can also use sugar substitutes to sweeten your ice cream, just be sure that the same amount of sweetness results from the alternative ingredient you choose. When I need a substitute for sugar, I generally choose stevia, which is a natural sugar alternative that comes in a liquid form. It can be found in many health food stores.

- I recommend using fresh fruit for all recipes, but frozen fruit can be used also. Just be sure to defrost the fruit thoroughly before incorporating it into the warm custard, so that the flavor of the fruit is fully absorbed.

- To freshen up ice cream that has been stored in the freezer for a few days (or even a few weeks), just place the ice cream in the refrigerator for about 20 minutes to soften, then put in the ice cream maker for a few spins. This will restore the ice cream's original texture and flavor. However, don't expect this to happen too often. In my house, homemade ice cream rarely lasts in the freezer for more than a day or two!

THE BASICS

The recipes below are simple to make, and simply delicious. Add your favorite ingredients to these basic recipes to make countless combinations and variations.

French Vanilla Ice Cream

(See picture on opposite page)

Makes 15 balls

1 1/2 cups whole milk

1/2 cup whipping cream

1 vanilla bean, split in half lengthwise

2/3 cup sugar

6 egg yolks

1. In a saucepan, bring the milk, cream, vanilla bean, and half of the sugar to the scalding point over medium heat.

2. In a bowl, beat the egg yolks and the remaining sugar with a wire whisk until smooth and uniform.

3. When the mixture in the saucepan begins to foam, reduce the heat and quickly stir in the yolk mixture. Remove the vanilla bean and scrape the seeds back into the saucepan.

4. Stirring constantly with a wooden spoon, cook the custard over low heat until it reaches 175°F.

5. Remove immediately from the heat and continue stirring, so that the custard does not overcook.

6. Pour the custard into a clean bowl through a fine mesh strainer, so that the liquid is smooth and lump-free.

7. Cover the custard with plastic wrap and let cool slightly, then place in the refrigerator for at least 4 hours, until very cold.

8. Transfer the cold custard to the bowl of your ice cream maker and process according to the manufacturer's instructions.

Vanilla Frozen Yogurt

Makes 15 balls

1 cup skim milk

1 vanilla bean, split in half lengthwise

2/3 cup natural brown sugar

6 egg yolks

1 cup liquid yogurt, minimum 3% fat

1. In a saucepan, bring the milk, vanilla bean, and half of the sugar to the scalding point over medium heat.

2. In a bowl, beat the egg yolks and the remaining sugar with a wire whisk until smooth and uniform.

3. When the mixture in the saucepan begins to foam, reduce the heat and quickly stir in the yolk mixture. Remove the vanilla bean and scrape the seeds back into the saucepan.

(Continued on page 12)

4. Stirring constantly with a wooden spoon, cook the custard over low heat until it reaches 175°F.

5. Remove immediately from the heat and continue stirring, so that the custard does not overcook.

6. Pour the custard into a clean bowl through a fine mesh strainer, so that the liquid is smooth and lump-free.

7. Pour in the yogurt and mix well.

8. Cover the custard with plastic wrap and let cool slightly, then place in the refrigerator to chill for at least 4 hours, until very cold.

9. Transfer the cold custard to the bowl of your ice cream maker and process according to the manufacturer's instructions until you have the desired texture.

Low-Fat Vanilla Frozen Yogurt

Makes 15 balls

1 cup skim milk

1 vanilla bean, split in half lengthwise

Sugar substitute equivalent to 3/4 cup sugar

6 egg yolks

1 1/2 cups low-fat liquid yogurt

1. In a saucepan, bring the milk, vanilla bean and half of the sugar substitute to the scalding point over medium heat.

2. In a bowl, beat the egg yolks and the remaining sugar substitute with a wire whisk until smooth and uniform.

3. When the mixture in the saucepan begins to foam, reduce the heat and quickly stir in the yolk mixture. Remove the vanilla bean and scrape the seeds back into the saucepan.

4. Stirring constantly with a wooden spoon, cook the custard over low heat until it reaches 175°F.

5. Remove immediately from the heat and continue stirring, so that the custard does not overcook.

6. Pour the custard into a clean bowl through a fine mesh strainer, so that the liquid is smooth and lump-free.

7. Pour in the yogurt and mix well.

8. Cover the custard with plastic wrap and let cool slightly, then place in the refrigerator for at least 4 hours, until very cold.

9. Transfer the cold custard to the bowl of your ice cream maker and process according to the manufacturer's instructions.

Vanilla Soya Milk Ice Cream

Makes 15 balls

2 cups soya milk

1 vanilla bean, split in half lengthwise

3/4 natural brown sugar

6 egg yolks

1. In a saucepan, bring the soya milk, vanilla bean, and half of the sugar to the scalding point over medium heat.
2. In a bowl, beat the egg yolks and the remaining sugar with a wire whisk until smooth and uniform.
3. When the mixture in the saucepan begins to foam, reduce the heat and quickly stir in the yolk mixture. Remove the vanilla bean and scrape the seeds back into the saucepan.
4. Stirring constantly with a wooden spoon, cook the custard over low heat until it reaches 175°F.
5. Remove immediately from the heat and continue stirring, so that the custard does not overcook.
6. Pour the custard into a clean bowl through a fine mesh strainer, so that the liquid is smooth and lump-free.
7. Cover the custard with plastic wrap and let cool slightly, then place in the refrigerator for at least 4 hours, until very cold.
8. Transfer the cold custard to the bowl of your ice cream maker and process according to the manufacturer's instructions.

Italian Vanilla Ice Cream

Makes 15 balls

1 cup whole milk

1 cup whipping cream

1 vanilla bean, split in half lengthwise

3/4 cup sugar

4 egg yolks

1. In a saucepan, bring the milk, cream, vanilla bean, and half of the sugar to the scalding point over medium heat.
2. In a bowl, beat the egg yolks and the remaining sugar with a wire whisk until smooth and uniform.
3. When the mixture in the saucepan begins to foam, reduce the heat and quickly stir in the yolk mixture. Remove the vanilla bean and scrape the seeds back into the saucepan.
4. Stirring constantly with a wooden spoon, cook the custard over low heat until it reaches 175°F.
5. Remove immediately from the heat and continue stirring, so that the custard does not overcook.
6. Pour the custard into a clean bowl through a fine mesh strainer, so that the liquid is smooth and lump-free.
7. Cover the custard with plastic wrap and let cool slightly, then place in the refrigerator for at least 4 hours, until very cold
8. Transfer the cold custard to the bowl of your ice cream maker and process according to the manufacturer's instructions.

CLASSICS

These flavors will remind you of summer afternoons at the local ice cream parlor. Serve with chocolate syrup, toasted nuts, whipped cream, or sprinkles.

Chocolate Fudge Ice Cream

(See picture on opposite page)

Makes 15 balls

1 1/2 cups whole milk

1 cup whipping cream

1 vanilla bean, split in half lengthwise

2/3 cup sugar

6 egg yolks

5 ounces bittersweet chocolate, cut into pieces

1. In a saucepan, bring the milk, 1/2 cup of the whipping cream, the vanilla bean, and half of the sugar to the scalding point over medium heat.

2. In a bowl, beat the egg yolks and the remaining sugar with a wire whisk until smooth and uniform.

3. When the mixture in the saucepan begins to foam, reduce the heat and quickly stir in the yolk mixture. Remove the vanilla bean and scrape the seeds back into the saucepan.

4. Using a wooden spoon, stir the custard constantly and cook over low heat until it reaches 175°F.

5. Remove immediately from the heat and continue stirring, so that the custard does not overcook.

6. Pour the custard into a clean bowl through a fine mesh strainer, so that the liquid is smooth and lump-free.

7. Cover the custard with plastic wrap and let cool slightly, then place in the refrigerator for at least 4 hours, until very cold.

8. In a small saucepan, heat the remaining 1/2 cup of whipping cream over medium heat until it reaches the boiling point. Remove from the heat, add the chocolate pieces and, using a wooden spoon, blend until smooth. Set aside so that the mixture cools slightly, but remains liquid.

9. Transfer the cold custard to the bowl of your ice cream maker and process according to the manufacturer's instructions, until the ice cream is hard.

10. Open the ice cream maker while it is operating, pour in the chocolate-whipping cream mixture, and operate for 2 more minutes.

Strawberry Ice Cream

(See picture on opposite page)

Makes 15 balls

1/2 cup whole milk

1 1/2 cups whipping cream

1 vanilla bean, split in half lengthwise

3/4 cup sugar

4 egg yolks

2/3 cup fresh strawberries, crushed with a fork

1. In a saucepan, bring the milk, cream, vanilla bean, and half of the sugar to the scalding point over medium heat.
2. In a bowl, beat the egg yolks and the remaining sugar with a wire whisk until smooth and uniform.
3. When the mixture in the saucepan begins to foam, reduce the heat and quickly stir in the yolk mixture. Remove the vanilla bean and scrape the seeds back into the saucepan.
4. Using a wooden spoon, stir the custard constantly and cook over low heat until it reaches 175°F.
5. Remove immediately from the heat and continue stirring, so that the custard does not overcook.
6. Pour the custard into a clean bowl through a fine mesh strainer, so that the liquid is smooth and lump-free. Set aside to cool to room temperature.
7. Add the crushed strawberries to the cooled custard and mix well. Cover with plastic wrap and place in the refrigerator for at least 4 hours, until very cold.
8. Transfer the cold custard to the bowl of your ice cream maker and process according to the manufacturer's instructions.

* *Replace strawberries with 2/3 cup fresh raspberries or peaches for a fruity variation.*

Dulce de Leche Ice Cream

Makes 15 balls

1 1/2 cups whole milk

1/2 cup whipping cream

1 vanilla bean, split in half lengthwise

2/3 cup sugar

6 egg yolks

1/2 cup dulce de leche

1. In a saucepan, bring the milk, cream, vanilla bean, and half of the sugar to the scalding point over medium heat.
2. In a bowl, beat the egg yolks and the remaining sugar with a wire whisk until smooth and uniform.
3. When the mixture in the saucepan begins to foam, reduce the heat and quickly stir in the yolk mixture. Remove the vanilla bean and scrape the seeds back into the saucepan.
4. Using a wooden spoon, stir the custard constantly and cook over low heat until it reaches 175°F.
5. Remove immediately from the heat and continue stirring, so that

(Continued on page18)

the custard does not overcook.

6. Pour the custard into a clean bowl through a fine mesh strainer, so that the liquid is smooth and lump-free.

7. While the custard is still warm, blend in the dulce de leche using a hand whisk. It is important to do this while the custard is warm so that the flavor is fully absorbed.

8. Cover the custard with plastic wrap and let cool slightly, then place in the refrigerator for at least 4 hours, until very cold.

9. Transfer the cold custard to the bowl of your ice cream maker and process according to the manufacturer's instructions.

* *Dulce de leche is a milk-based caramel spread popular in South America. It can be found in specialty food stores and fine supermarkets.*

Cocoa Almond Ice Cream

(See picture on opposite page)

Makes 15 balls

1 1/2 cups whole milk

1/2 cup whipping cream

1 vanilla bean, split in half lengthwise

2/3 cup sugar

6 egg yolks

1/2 cup slivered blanched almonds

2 tablespoons cocoa

1. In a saucepan, bring the milk, cream, vanilla bean, and half of the sugar to the scalding point over medium heat.

2. In a bowl, beat the egg yolks and the remaining sugar with a wire whisk until smooth and uniform.

3. When the mixture in the saucepan begins to foam, reduce the heat and quickly stir in the yolk mixture. Remove the vanilla bean and scrape the seeds back into the saucepan.

4. Using a wooden spoon, stir the custard constantly and cook over low heat until it reaches 175°F.

5. Remove immediately from the heat and continue stirring, so that the custard does not overcook.

6. Pour the custard into a clean bowl through a fine mesh strainer, so that the liquid is smooth and lump-free.

7. While the custard is still warm, add the almonds and mix well.

8. Cover the custard with plastic wrap and let cool slightly, then place in the refrigerator for at least 4 hours, until very cold.

9. Transfer the cold custard to the bowl of your ice cream maker and process according to the manufacturer's instructions, until the ice cream is hard.

10. Open the ice cream maker while it is operating and add 1 tablespoon of cocoa. Allow the machine to operate for 1 minute, then add the other tablespoon of cocoa. Let the machine continue to operate for 3 turns and then turn it off.

Mint Ice Cream

(See picture on opposite page)

Makes 15 balls

1 cup whole milk

1 cup whipping cream

1 vanilla bean, split in half lengthwise

3/4 cup sugar

4 egg yolks

1/4 cup mint liqueur

1. In a saucepan, bring the milk, cream, vanilla bean, and half of the sugar to the scalding point over medium heat.
2. In a bowl, beat the egg yolks and the remaining sugar with a wire whisk until smooth and uniform.
3. When the mixture in the saucepan begins to foam, reduce the heat and quickly stir in the yolk mixture. Remove the vanilla bean and scrape the seeds back into the saucepan.
4. Using a wooden spoon, stir the custard constantly and cook over low heat until it reaches 175°F.
5. Remove immediately from the heat and continue stirring, so that the custard does not overcook.
6. Pour the custard into a clean bowl through a fine mesh strainer, so that the liquid is smooth and lump-free.
7. While the custard is still warm, add the mint liqueur and mix well. It is important to do this while the custard is warm so that the flavor is fully absorbed.
8. Cover the custard with plastic wrap and let cool slightly, then place in the refrigerator for at least 4 hours, until very cold.
9. Transfer the cold custard to the bowl of your ice cream maker and process according to the manufacturer's instructions.

* *To make Irish Cream Ice Cream, replace mint liqueur with 1/2 cup Irish Cream.*

Espresso Ice Cream

Makes 15 balls

1 cup whole milk

1 cup whipping cream

1 vanilla bean, split in half lengthwise

3/4 cup sugar

4 egg yolks

1/4 cup strong espresso

1 tablespoon ground espresso beans

1. In a saucepan, bring the milk, cream, vanilla bean, and half of the sugar to the scalding point over medium heat.
2. In a bowl, beat the egg yolks and the remaining sugar with a wire whisk until smooth and uniform.
3. When the mixture in the saucepan begins to foam, reduce the heat and quickly stir in the yolk mixture. Remove the vanilla bean and scrape the seeds back into the saucepan.
4. Using a wooden spoon, stir the custard constantly and cook over low heat until it reaches 175°F.

(Continued on page 22)

5. Remove immediately from the heat and continue stirring, so that the custard does not overcook.

6. Pour the custard into a clean bowl through a fine mesh strainer, so that the liquid is smooth and lump-free.

7. While the custard is still warm, add the espresso and ground espresso beans and mix well. It is important to do this while the custard is warm so that the coffee flavor is fully absorbed.

8. Cover the custard with plastic wrap and let cool slightly, then place in the refrigerator for at least 4 hours, until very cold.

9. Transfer the cold custard to the bowl of your ice cream maker and process according to the manufacturer's instructions.

* *I recommend using fresh espresso prepared in an espresso machine or stovetop espresso maker. To make Espresso Frangelico Ice Cream, replace ground espresso beans with 2 tablespoons Frangelico liqueur.*

Cookies and Coffee Ice Cream

(See picture on opposite page)

Makes 15 balls

1 cup whole milk

1 cup whipping cream

1 vanilla bean, split in half lengthwise

3/4 cup sugar

4 egg yolks

1/4 cup strong espresso

1/2 cup coarsely chopped chocolate cookies

1. In a saucepan, bring the milk, cream, vanilla bean, and half of the sugar to the scalding point over medium heat.

2. In a bowl, beat the egg yolks and the remaining sugar with a wire whisk until smooth and uniform.

3. When the mixture in the saucepan begins to foam, reduce the heat and quickly stir in the yolk mixture. Remove the vanilla bean and scrape the seeds back into the saucepan.

4. Using a wooden spoon, stir the custard constantly and cook over low heat until it reaches 175°F.

5. Remove immediately from the heat and continue stirring, so that the custard does not overcook.

6. Pour the custard into a clean bowl through a fine mesh strainer, so that the liquid is smooth and lump-free.

7. Add the espresso and mix well. It is important to do this while the custard is warm so that the flavor is fully absorbed.

8. Cover the custard with plastic wrap and let cool slightly, then place in the refrigerator for at least 4 hours, until very cold.

9. Transfer the cold custard to the bowl of your ice cream maker, add the cookie pieces, and process according to the manufacturer's instructions.

Chocolate Ice Cream with Rainbow Chips

(See picture on opposite page)

Makes 15 balls

1 cup whole milk

1 cup whipping cream

1 vanilla bean, split in half lengthwise

3/4 cup sugar

6 egg yolks

5 ounces bittersweet chocolate, cut into small pieces

3 ounces candy-covered chocolate candies (about 2 small packages)

1. In a saucepan, bring the milk, cream, vanilla bean, and half of the sugar to the scalding point over medium heat.

2. In a bowl, beat the egg yolks and the remaining sugar with a wire whisk until smooth and uniform.

3. When the mixture in the saucepan begins to foam, reduce the heat and quickly stir in the yolk mixture. Remove the vanilla bean and scrape the seeds back into the saucepan.

4. Using a wooden spoon, stir the custard constantly and cook over low heat until it reaches 175°F.

5. Remove immediately from the heat and continue stirring, so that the custard does not overcook.

6. Pour the custard into a clean bowl through a fine mesh strainer, so that the liquid is smooth and lump-free. Quickly add the bittersweet chocolate and mix well until all the chocolate has melted.

7. Cover the custard with plastic wrap and let cool slightly, then place in the refrigerator for at least 4 hours, until very cold.

8. Transfer the cold custard to the bowl of your ice cream maker. Add the chocolate candies and process according to the manufacturer's instructions, until the ice cream is hard.

Tiramisu Ice Cream

Makes 15 balls

1 cup whole milk

1 cup whipping cream

1 vanilla bean, split in half lengthwise

3/4 cup sugar

8 egg yolks

1/3 cup mascarpone cheese

3 tablespoons strong espresso

2 tablespoons amaretto

1. In a saucepan, bring the milk, cream, vanilla bean, and half of the sugar to the scalding point over medium heat.

2. In a bowl, beat the egg yolks and the remaining sugar with a wire whisk until smooth and uniform.

3. When the mixture in the saucepan begins to foam, reduce the heat and quickly stir in the yolk mixture. Remove the vanilla bean and scrape the seeds back into the saucepan.

4. Stirring constantly with a wooden spoon, cook the custard over low heat until it reaches 175°F.

5. Remove immediately from the heat and continue stirring, so that the custard does not overcook.

(Continued on page 26)

6. Pour the custard into a clean bowl through a fine mesh strainer, so that the liquid is smooth and lump-free.

7. While the custard is still warm, add the mascarpone, espresso and amaretto and mix well. It is important to do this while the custard is warm so that the flavors are fully absorbed.

8. Cover the custard with plastic wrap and let cool slightly, then place in the refrigerator for at least 4 hours, until very cold.

9. Transfer the cold custard to the bowl of your ice cream maker and process according to the manufacturer's instructions.

Rum Raisin Ice Cream

Makes 15 balls

1/2 cup golden raisins

3 tablespoons rum

1 1/2 cups whole milk

1/2 cup whipping cream

1 vanilla bean, split in half lengthwise

2/3 cup sugar

6 egg yolks

1. Soak the raisins in the rum for at least 2 hours.

2. In a saucepan, bring the milk, cream, vanilla bean, and half of the sugar to the scalding point over medium heat.

3. In a bowl, beat the egg yolks and the remaining sugar with a wire whisk until smooth and uniform.

4. When the mixture in the saucepan begins to foam, reduce the heat and quickly stir in the yolk mixture. Remove the vanilla bean and scrape the seeds back into the saucepan.

5. Using a wooden spoon, stir the custard constantly and cook over low heat until it reaches 175°F.

6. Remove immediately from the heat and continue stirring, so that the custard does not overcook.

7. Pour the custard into a clean bowl through a fine mesh strainer, so that the liquid is smooth and lump-free.

8. Cover the custard with plastic wrap and let cool slightly, then place in the refrigerator for at least 4 hours, until very cold.

9. Transfer the cold custard to the bowl of your ice cream maker, add the rum-soaked raisins, and process according to the manufacturer's instructions.

Candied Almond Ice Cream

Makes 15 balls

Candied Almonds
1/4 cup sugar

1/2 cup coarsely chopped blanched almonds

1/2 tablespoon oil

Ice Cream
1 cup whole milk

1 cup whipping cream

1 vanilla bean, split in half lengthwise

2/3 cup sugar

4 egg yolks

1. In a heavy skillet, cook the sugar over medium heat until caramelized and golden.

2. Reduce the heat to low, add the almonds, and continue cooking until the almonds are a golden brown color.

3. Grease a large porcelain serving dish with the oil and pour out the almonds onto the dish. Set aside for 30 minutes.

4. Separately, in a saucepan, bring the milk, cream, vanilla bean, and half of the sugar to the scalding point over medium heat.

5. In a bowl, beat the egg yolks and the remaining sugar with a wire whisk until smooth and uniform.

6. When the mixture in the saucepan begins to foam, reduce the heat and quickly stir in the yolk mixture. Remove the vanilla bean and scrape the seeds back into the saucepan.

7. Using a wooden spoon, stir the custard constantly and cook over low heat until it reaches 175°F.

8. Remove immediately from the heat and continue stirring, so that the custard does not overcook.

9. Pour the custard into a clean bowl through a fine mesh strainer, so that the liquid is smooth and lump-free.

10. Place the candied almonds in a food processor and process until ground. Pour into the custard while the custard is still warm, and mix well. It is important to do this while the custard is warm so that the flavors are fully absorbed.

11. Cover the custard with plastic wrap and let cool slightly, then place in the refrigerator for at least 4 hours, until very cold.

12. Transfer the cold custard to the bowl of your ice cream maker and process according to the manufacturer's instructions.

NATURALLY DELICIOUS

Coconut milk, toasted granola, natural peanut butter and wildflower honey are just some of the wholesome ingredients in these recipes.

Raspberry Ice Cream

(See picture on opposite page)

Makes 15 balls

1 cup whole milk

1 cup whipping cream

1 vanilla bean, split in half lengthwise

3/4 cup sugar

4 egg yolks

6 ounces raspberries, fresh or frozen and thawed

1. In a saucepan, bring the milk, cream, vanilla bean, and half of the sugar to the scalding point over medium heat.
2. In a bowl, beat the egg yolks and the remaining sugar with a wire whisk until smooth and uniform.
3. When the mixture in the saucepan begins to foam, reduce the heat and quickly stir in the yolk mixture. Remove the vanilla bean and scrape the seeds back into the saucepan.
4. Using a wooden spoon, stir the custard constantly and cook over low heat until it reaches 175°F.
5. Remove immediately from the heat and continue stirring, so that the custard does not overcook.
6. Pour the custard into a clean bowl through a fine mesh strainer, so that the liquid is smooth and lump-free.
7. Cover the custard with plastic wrap and let cool slightly, then place in the refrigerator for at least 4 hours, until very cold.
8. Transfer the cold custard to the bowl of your ice cream maker, add the raspberries, and process according to the manufacturer's instructions.

* *To make Blueberry Ice Cream, replace raspberries with 6 ounces blueberries.*

Peanut Butter Ice Cream

Makes 15 balls

1 1/2 cups whole milk

1/2 cup whipping cream

1 vanilla bean, split in half lengthwise

2/3 cup sugar

6 egg yolks

1/2 cup smooth natural peanut butter

1. In a saucepan, bring the milk, cream, vanilla bean, and half of the sugar to the scalding point over medium heat.
2. In a bowl, beat the egg yolks and the remaining sugar with a wire whisk until smooth and uniform.
3. When the mixture in the saucepan begins to foam, reduce the heat and quickly stir in the yolk mixture. Remove the vanilla bean and scrape the seeds back into the saucepan.
4. Using a wooden spoon, stir the custard constantly and cook over low heat until it reaches 175°F.
5. Remove immediately from the heat and continue stirring, so that the custard does not overcook.
6. Pour the custard into a clean bowl through a fine mesh strainer, so that the liquid is smooth and lump-free.
7. While the custard is still warm, add the peanut butter and mix well. It is important to do this while the custard is warm so that the flavors are fully absorbed.
8. Cover the custard with plastic wrap and let cool slightly, then place in the refrigerator for at least 4 hours, until very cold.
9. Transfer the cold custard to the bowl of your ice cream maker and process according to the manufacturer's instructions.

Plum Ice Cream

Makes 15 balls

1/2 cup fresh plums, pitted and finely chopped

1 tablespoon red port wine

1 cup whole milk

1 cup whipping cream

1 vanilla bean, split in half lengthwise

3/4 cup sugar

4 egg yolks

1. Soak the plums in the wine for 1 hour.
2. Separately, in a saucepan, bring the milk, cream, vanilla bean, and half of the sugar to the scalding point over medium heat.
3. In a bowl, beat the egg yolks and the remaining sugar with a wire whisk until smooth and uniform.
4. When the mixture in the saucepan begins to foam, reduce the heat and quickly stir in the yolk mixture. Remove the vanilla bean and scrape the seeds back into the saucepan.
5. Using a wooden spoon, stir the custard constantly and cook over low heat until it reaches 175°F.
6. Remove immediately from the heat and continue stirring, so that the custard does not overcook.
7. Pour the custard into a clean bowl through a fine mesh strainer, so that the liquid is smooth and lump-free.

8. While the custard is still warm, pour in the soaked plums and mix well. It is important to do this while the custard is warm so that the flavors are fully absorbed.

9. Cover the custard with plastic wrap and let cool slightly, then place in the refrigerator for at least 4 hours, until very cold.

10. Transfer the cold custard to the bowl of your ice cream maker and process according to the manufacturer's instructions.

Caramel Apple Ice Cream

Makes 15 balls

Caramel Apples
1/3 cup sugar

2 Granny Smith apples, peeled, cored, and finely chopped

Ice Cream
1 cup whole milk

1 cup whipping cream

1 vanilla bean, split in half lengthwise

3/4 cup sugar

4 egg yolks

1. In a heavy skillet, place 1/3 cup sugar and cook on medium heat, without stirring, until caramelized and light brown.

2. Remove from the heat and stir in the chopped apples, mixing with a wooden spoon for about 2 minutes.

3. Return to the heat and cook over low heat for 15 minutes, stirring constantly with the wooden spoon, until all the apple pieces have a caramel color.

4. Remove from the heat and set aside.

5. Separately, in a saucepan, bring the milk, cream, vanilla bean, and half of the sugar to the scalding point over medium heat.

6. In a bowl, beat the egg yolks and the remaining sugar with a wire whisk until smooth and uniform.

7. When the mixture in the saucepan begins to foam, reduce the heat and quickly stir in the yolk mixture. Remove the vanilla bean and scrape the seeds back into the saucepan.

8. Using a wooden spoon, stir the custard constantly and cook over low heat until it reaches 175°F.

9. Remove immediately from the heat and continue stirring, so that the custard does not overcook.

10. Pour the custard into a clean bowl through a fine mesh strainer, so that the liquid is smooth and lump-free.

11. While the custard is still warm, add the caramel apples and mix well. It is important to do this while the custard is warm so that the flavor is fully absorbed.

12. Cover the custard with plastic wrap and let cool slightly, then place in the refrigerator for at least 4 hours, until very cold.

13. Transfer the cold custard to the bowl of your ice cream maker and process according to the manufacturer's instructions.

Granola Ice Cream

(See picture on opposite page)

Makes 15 balls

1 cup whole milk

1 cup whipping cream

1 vanilla bean, split in half lengthwise

3/4 cup sugar

5 egg yolks

1/2 cup toasted granola

1. In a saucepan, bring the milk, cream, vanilla bean, and half of the sugar to the scalding point over medium heat.

2. In a bowl, beat the egg yolks and the remaining sugar with a wire whisk until smooth and uniform.

3. When the mixture in the saucepan begins to foam, reduce the heat and quickly stir in the yolk mixture. Remove the vanilla bean and scrape the seeds back into the saucepan.

4. Using a wooden spoon, stir the custard constantly and cook over low heat until it reaches 175°F.

5. Remove immediately from the heat and continue stirring, so that the custard does not overcook.

6. Pour the custard into a clean bowl through a fine mesh strainer, so that the liquid is smooth and lump-free.

7. Cover the custard with plastic wrap and let cool slightly, then place in the refrigerator for at least 4 hours, until very cold.

8. Transfer the cold custard to the bowl of your ice cream maker. Add the granola and process according to the manufacturer's instructions until hard.

Honey Banana Ice Cream

Makes 15 balls

1/4 cup wildflower or orange blossom honey

2 large ripe bananas, cut into 1/8-inch slices

1 cup whole milk

1 cup whipping cream

1 vanilla bean, split in half lengthwise

3/4 cup sugar

4 egg yolks

1. In a heavy skillet, heat half of the honey over medium heat.

2. When the honey starts to bubble, mix in the banana slices using a wooden spoon, and cook for another 5 minutes. Turn off the heat and put the mixture aside.

3. In a separate saucepan, bring the milk, cream, vanilla bean, and half of the sugar to the scalding point over medium heat.

4. In a bowl, beat the egg yolks and the remaining sugar with a wire whisk until smooth and uniform.

5. When the mixture in the saucepan begins to foam, reduce the heat and quickly stir in the yolk mixture. Remove the vanilla bean and scrape the seeds back into the saucepan.

6. Using a wooden spoon, stir the custard constantly and cook over low heat until it reaches 175°F.

(Continued on page 34)

7. Remove immediately from the heat and continue stirring, so that the custard does not overcook.

8. Pour the custard into a clean bowl through a fine mesh strainer, so that the liquid is smooth and lump-free.

9. While the custard is still warm, add the cooked bananas and the remaining honey and mix well. It is important to do this while the custard is warm so that the flavors are fully absorbed.

10. Cover the custard with plastic wrap and let cool slightly, then place in the refrigerator for at least 4 hours, until very cold.

11. Transfer the cold custard to the bowl of your ice cream maker and process according to the manufacturer's instructions.

Roasted Pineapple Ice Cream

Makes 15 balls

Roasted Pineapple
1 pineapple, peeled and cut into 1/2-inch cubes

1/3 cup sugar

Ice Cream
1 cup whole milk

1 cup whipping cream

1 vanilla bean, split in half lengthwise

3/4 cup sugar

4 egg yolks

1. Preheat the oven to 400°F. Line a baking sheet with aluminum foil.

2. In a bowl, mix the pineapple and the sugar. Transfer to the lined baking sheet and cook for 25 minutes. Remove, drain the excess liquid, and set aside.

3. In a saucepan, bring the milk, cream, vanilla bean, and half of the sugar to the scalding point over medium heat.

4. In a bowl, beat the egg yolks and the remaining sugar with a wire whisk until smooth and uniform.

5. When the mixture in the saucepan begins to foam, reduce the heat and quickly stir in the yolk mixture. Remove the vanilla bean and scrape the seeds back into the saucepan.

6. Using a wooden spoon, stir the custard constantly and cook over low heat until it reaches 175°F.

7. Remove immediately from the heat and continue stirring, so that the custard does not overcook.

8. Pour the custard into a clean bowl through a fine mesh strainer, so that the liquid is smooth and lump-free.

9. While the custard is still warm, add the roasted pineapple cubes and mix well. It is important to do this while the custard is warm so that the flavors are fully absorbed.

10. Cover the custard with plastic wrap and let cool slightly, then place in the refrigerator for at least 4 hours, until very cold.

11. Transfer the cold custard to the bowl of your ice cream maker and process according to the manufacturer's instructions.

Piña Colada Ice Cream

Makes 15 balls

1 cup coconut milk

1 1/2 cups whipping cream

1 vanilla bean, split in half lengthwise

3/4 cup sugar

4 egg yolks

1/4 cup piña colada mix

1. In a saucepan, bring the coconut milk, cream, vanilla bean, and half of the sugar to the scalding point over medium heat.
2. In a bowl, beat the egg yolks and the remaining sugar with a wire whisk until smooth and uniform.
3. When the mixture in the saucepan begins to foam, reduce the heat and quickly stir in the yolk mixture. Remove the vanilla bean and scrape the seeds back into the saucepan.
4. Using a wooden spoon, stir the custard constantly and cook over low heat until it reaches 175°F.
5. Remove immediately from the heat and continue stirring, so that the custard does not overcook.
6. Pour the custard into a clean bowl through a fine mesh strainer, so that the liquid is smooth and lump-free.
7. While the custard is still warm, pour in the piña colada and mix well. It is important to do this while the custard is warm so that the flavors are fully absorbed.
8. Cover the custard with plastic wrap and let cool slightly, then place in the refrigerator for at least 4 hours, until very cold.
9. Transfer the cold custard to the bowl of your ice cream maker and process according to the manufacturer's instructions.

Ginger Ice Cream

Makes 15 balls

1 cup whole milk

1 cup whipping cream

1 vanilla bean, split in half lengthwise

3/4 cup sugar

4 egg yolks

1/2 cup coarsely chopped candied ginger

1. In a saucepan, bring the milk, cream, vanilla bean, and half of the sugar to the scalding point over medium heat.
2. In a bowl, beat the egg yolks and the remaining sugar with a wire whisk until smooth and uniform.
3. When the mixture in the saucepan begins to foam, reduce the heat and quickly stir in the yolk mixture. Remove the vanilla bean and scrape the seeds back into the saucepan.
4. Using a wooden spoon, stir the custard constantly and cook over low heat until it reaches 175°F.
5. Remove immediately from the heat and continue stirring, so that the custard does not overcook.

(Continued on next page)

6. Pour the custard into a clean bowl through a fine mesh strainer, so that the liquid is smooth and lump-free.

7. While the custard is still warm, add the candied ginger and mix well. It is important to do this while the custard is warm so that the flavors are fully absorbed.

8. Cover the custard with plastic wrap and let cool slightly, then place in the refrigerator for at least 4 hours, until very cold.

9. Transfer the cold custard to the bowl of your ice cream maker and process according to the manufacturer's instructions.

Honey and Spice Ice Cream

(See picture on opposite page)

Makes 15 balls

1 1/2 cups whole milk

1/2 cup whipping cream

1 vanilla bean, split in half lengthwise

1/2 cup honey

1/2 cup sugar

6 egg yolks

1/2 teaspoon ground cinnamon

1/2 teaspoon ground nutmeg

1. In a saucepan, bring the milk, cream, vanilla bean, honey, and half of the sugar to the scalding point over medium heat.

2. In a bowl, beat the egg yolks and the remaining sugar with a wire whisk until smooth and uniform.

3. When the mixture in the saucepan begins to foam, reduce the heat and quickly stir in the yolk mixture. Remove the vanilla bean and scrape the seeds back into the saucepan.

4. Using a wooden spoon, stir the custard constantly and cook over low heat until it reaches 175°F.

5. Remove immediately from the heat and continue stirring, so that the custard does not overcook.

6. Pour the custard into a clean bowl through a fine mesh strainer, so that the liquid is smooth and lump-free.

7. While the custard is still warm, add the cinnamon and nutmeg and mix well. It is important to do this while the custard is warm so that the flavors are fully absorbed.

8. Cover the custard with plastic wrap and let cool slightly, then place in the refrigerator for at least 4 hours, until very cold.

9. Transfer the cold custard to the bowl of your ice cream maker and process according to the manufacturer's instructions.

Earl Grey Ice Cream

Makes 15 balls

1 cup whole milk

2 tablespoons loose Earl Grey tea

1 cup whipping cream

1 vanilla bean, split in half lengthwise

3/4 cup sugar

4 egg yolks

1. In a saucepan, bring the milk, tea, cream, vanilla bean, and half of the sugar to the scalding point over medium heat.
2. In a bowl, beat the egg yolks and the remaining sugar with a wire whisk until smooth and uniform.
3. When the mixture in the saucepan begins to foam, reduce the heat and quickly stir in the yolk mixture. Remove the vanilla bean and scrape the seeds back into the saucepan.
4. Using a wooden spoon, stir the custard constantly and cook over low heat until it reaches 175°F.
5. Remove immediately from the heat and continue stirring, so that the custard does not overcook.
6. Pour the custard into a clean bowl through a fine mesh strainer, so that the liquid is smooth and lump-free.
7. Cover the custard with plastic wrap and let cool slightly, then place in the refrigerator for at least 4 hours, until very cold.
8. Transfer the cold custard to the bowl of your ice cream maker and process according to the manufacturer's instructions.

Carob Vanilla Ice Cream

Makes 15 balls

1 cup whole milk

1 cup whipping cream

1 vanilla bean, split in half lengthwise

3/4 cup sugar

5 egg yolks

6 ounces carob, grated or finely ground

1. In a saucepan, bring the milk, cream, vanilla bean, and half of the sugar to the scalding point over medium heat.
2. In a bowl, beat the egg yolks and the remaining sugar with a wire whisk until smooth and uniform.
3. When the mixture in the saucepan begins to foam, reduce the heat and quickly stir in the yolk mixture. Remove the vanilla bean and scrape the seeds back into the saucepan.
4. Using a wooden spoon, stir the custard constantly and cook over low heat until it reaches 175°F.
5. Remove immediately from the heat and continue stirring, so that the custard does not overcook.
6. Pour the custard into a clean bowl through a fine mesh strainer, so that the liquid is smooth and lump-free.
7. Cover the custard with plastic wrap and let cool slightly, then place in the refrigerator for at least 4 hours, until very cold.
8. Mix the carob into the cold custard. Transfer to the bowl of your ice cream maker and process according to the manufacturer's instructions.

Pecan Ice Cream

Makes 15 balls

1 1/2 cups whole milk

1/2 cup whipping cream

1 vanilla bean, split in half lengthwise

3/4 cup sugar

6 egg yolks

1/2 cup coarsely chopped candied pecans

1. In a saucepan, bring the milk, cream, vanilla bean, and half of the sugar to the scalding point over medium heat.
2. In a bowl, beat the egg yolks and the remaining sugar with a wire whisk until smooth and uniform.
3. When the mixture in the saucepan begins to foam, reduce the heat and quickly stir in the yolk mixture. Remove the vanilla bean and scrape the seeds back into the saucepan.
4. Stirring constantly with a wooden spoon, cook the custard over low heat until it reaches 175°F.
5. Remove immediately from the heat and continue stirring, so that the custard does not overcook.
6. Pour the custard into a clean bowl through a fine mesh strainer, so that the liquid is smooth and lump-free.
7. While the custard is still warm, add the candied pecans and mix well. It is important to do this while the custard is warm so that the flavor is fully absorbed.
8. Cover the custard with plastic wrap and let cool slightly, then place in the refrigerator for at least 4 hours, until very cold.
9. Transfer the cold custard to the bowl of your ice cream maker and process according to the manufacturer's instructions.

* Candied pecans can be found in natural food stores and candy shops.

Rose Water Ice Cream

Makes 15 balls

1 cup whole milk

1 cup whipping cream

1 vanilla bean, split in half lengthwise

2 tablespoons rose water

3/4 cup sugar

4 egg yolks

1. In a saucepan, bring the milk, cream, vanilla bean, rose water, and half of the sugar to the scalding point over medium heat.
2. In a bowl, beat the egg yolks and the remaining sugar with a wire whisk until smooth and uniform.
3. When the mixture in the saucepan begins to foam, reduce the heat and quickly stir in the yolk mixture. Remove the vanilla bean and scrape the seeds back into the saucepan.
4. Using a wooden spoon, stir the custard constantly and cook over low heat until it reaches 175°F.
5. Remove immediately from the heat and continue stirring, so that the custard does not overcook.

(Continued on page 40)

6. Pour the custard into a clean bowl through a fine mesh strainer, so that the liquid is smooth and lump-free.

7. Cover the custard with plastic wrap and let cool slightly, then place in the refrigerator for at least 4 hours, until very cold.

8. Transfer the cold custard to the bowl of your ice cream maker and process according to the manufacturer's instructions.

* *Rose water is a delicate flavoring that can be found in Middle Eastern food stores and specialty shops.*

Kumquat Ice Cream

(See picture on opposite page)

Makes 15 balls

Candied Kumquats
1/2 pound kumquats

1 cup sugar

Ice Cream
1 1/2 cups whole milk

1/2 cup whipping cream

1 vanilla bean, split in half lengthwise

2/3 cup sugar

6 egg yolks

1. Wash the kumquats thoroughly and place in a small pot. Cover with water and boil for 15 minutes. Drain the kumquats, cover with fresh water, and boil again. Repeat once more to remove the fruit's natural bitter flavor.

2. After boiling and draining for the third time, transfer the kumquats to a small saucepan. Add the sugar and cook covered for 45 minutes over low heat. Remove the cover and continue cooking for another 45 minutes. Set aside to cool and then chop into small pieces.

3. Separately, in a saucepan, bring the milk, cream, vanilla bean, and half of the sugar to the scalding point over medium heat.

4. In a bowl, beat the egg yolks and the remaining sugar with a wire whisk until smooth and uniform.

5. When the mixture in the saucepan begins to foam, reduce the heat and quickly stir in the yolk mixture. Remove the vanilla bean and scrape the seeds back into the saucepan.

6. Using a wooden spoon, stir the custard constantly and cook over low heat until it reaches 175°F.

7. Remove immediately from the heat and continue stirring, so that the custard does not overcook.

8. Pour the custard into a clean bowl through a fine mesh strainer, so that the liquid is smooth and lump-free.

9. While the custard is still warm, add the candied kumquats and mix well. It is important to do this while the custard is warm so that the flavors are fully absorbed.

10. Cover the custard with plastic wrap and let cool slightly, then place in the refrigerator for at least 4 hours, until very cold.

11. Transfer the cold custard to the bowl of your ice cream maker and process according to the manufacturer's instructions.

SOMETHING DIFFERENT

If you never thought of putting balsamic vinegar, white wine or mascarpone cheese in ice cream—think again. The innovations in this section will surprise and delight your taste buds.

Balsamic Ice Cream

(See picture on opposite page)

Makes 15 balls

1/2 cup balsamic vinegar

1 cup whole milk

1 cup whipping cream

1 vanilla bean, split in half lengthwise

3/4 cup sugar

4 egg yolks

1. Place the vinegar in a small saucepan and bring to the boiling point over medium heat.

2. When the vinegar boils, reduce the heat to low and continue cooking until the vinegar thickens to the consistency of chocolate syrup. Remove from the heat and set aside.

3. In another saucepan, bring the milk, cream, vanilla bean, and half of the sugar to the scalding point over medium heat.

4. In a bowl, beat the egg yolks and the remaining sugar with a wire whisk until smooth and uniform.

5. When the mixture in the saucepan begins to foam, reduce the heat and quickly stir in the yolk mixture. Remove the vanilla bean and scrape the seeds back into the saucepan.

6. Using a wooden spoon, stir the custard constantly and cook over low heat until it reaches 175°F.

7. Remove immediately from the heat and continue stirring, so that the custard does not overcook.

8. Pour the custard into a clean bowl through a fine mesh strainer, so that the liquid is smooth and lump-free.

9. Cover the custard with plastic wrap and let cool slightly, then place in the refrigerator for at least 4 hours, until very cold.

10. To make an ice cream with uniform color, add the vinegar to the cold custard and mix well. Transfer to the bowl of your ice cream maker and process according to the manufacturer's instructions until hard.

    To make a streaked ice cream, don't add the vinegar until the custard has been processed in the ice cream maker until soft. At this stage, open the ice cream maker while it is operating and pour in the vinegar slowly and unevenly. After you have poured in all the vinegar, close the ice cream maker and continue to operate until the texture is hard.

Marzipan Ice Cream

Makes 15 balls

1 cup whole milk

1 cup whipping cream

1 vanilla bean, split in half lengthwise

6 ounces marzipan

3/4 cup sugar

4 egg yolks

1 tablespoon amaretto

1. In a saucepan, bring the milk, cream, vanilla bean, marzipan, and half of the sugar to the scalding point over medium heat.

2. In a bowl, beat the egg yolks and the remaining sugar with a wire whisk until smooth and uniform.

3. When the mixture in the saucepan begins to foam, reduce the heat and quickly stir in the yolk mixture. Remove the vanilla bean and scrape the seeds back into the saucepan.

4. Using a wooden spoon, stir the custard constantly and cook over low heat until it reaches 175°F.

5. Remove immediately from the heat and continue stirring, so that the custard does not overcook.

6. Pour the custard into a clean bowl through a fine mesh strainer, so that the liquid is smooth and lump-free.

7. While the custard is still warm, add the amaretto and mix well. It is important to do this while the custard is warm so that the flavor is fully absorbed.

8. Cover the custard with plastic wrap and let cool slightly, then place in the refrigerator for at least 4 hours, until very cold.

9. Transfer the cold custard to the bowl of your ice cream maker and process according to the manufacturer's instructions.

Chocolate Brandy Ice Cream

Makes 15 balls

1/2 cup whole milk

1 1/2 cup whipping cream

1 vanilla bean, split in half lengthwise

3/4 cup sugar

4 egg yolks

5 ounces bittersweet chocolate, cut into small pieces

1 tablespoon brandy

1. In a saucepan, bring the milk, cream, vanilla bean, and half of the sugar to the scalding point over medium heat.

2. In a bowl, beat the egg yolks and the remaining sugar with a wire whisk until smooth and uniform.

3. When the mixture in the saucepan begins to foam, reduce the heat and quickly stir in the yolk mixture. Remove the vanilla bean and scrape the seeds back into the saucepan.

4. Using a wooden spoon, stir the custard constantly and cook over low heat until it reaches 175°F.

5. Remove immediately from the heat and continue stirring, so that the custard does not overcook.

6. Pour the custard into a clean bowl through a fine mesh strainer, so that the liquid is smooth and lump-free.

7. While the custard is still warm, mix in the chocolate pieces until all the chocolate has melted. Add the brandy and mix well.

8. Cover the custard with plastic wrap and let cool slightly, then place in the refrigerator for at least 4 hours, until very cold.

9. Transfer the cold custard to the bowl of your ice cream maker and process according to the manufacturer's instructions.

* *Omit brandy to make a rich and creamy Chocolate Ice Cream. To make Chocolate Whiskey Ice Cream, replace brandy with 3 tablespoons fine whiskey.*

Nougat Ice Cream

Makes 15 balls

1 1/2 cups whole milk

1/2 cup whipping cream

1 vanilla bean, split in half lengthwise

2/3 cup sugar

6 egg yolks

6 ounces almond nougat, coarsely chopped

1. In a saucepan, bring the milk, cream, vanilla bean, and half of the sugar to the scalding point over medium heat.

2. In a bowl, beat the egg yolks and the remaining sugar with a wire whisk until smooth and uniform.

3. When the mixture in the saucepan begins to foam, reduce the heat and quickly stir in the yolk mixture. Remove the vanilla bean and scrape the seeds back into the saucepan.

4. Using a wooden spoon, stir the custard constantly and cook over low heat until it reaches 175°F.

5. Remove immediately from the heat and continue stirring, so that the custard does not overcook.

6. Pour the custard into a clean bowl through a fine mesh strainer, so that the liquid is smooth and lump-free.

7. While the custard is still warm, add the almond nougat and mix well. It is important to do this while the custard is warm so that the flavors are fully absorbed.

8. Cover the custard with plastic wrap and let cool slightly, then place in the refrigerator for at least 4 hours, until very cold.

9. Transfer the cold custard to the bowl of your ice cream maker and process according to the manufacturer's instructions.

* *Nougat is a confectionary made from honey and nuts. It can be found in specialty food stores and candy shops.*

Zabaione Ice Cream

(See picture on opposite page)

Makes 15 balls

5 egg yolks

1/4 cup water

1/2 cup sugar

1 cup whipping cream

1. In the bowl of a standing mixer, place the egg yolks and whip on medium speed.

2. In the meantime, in a small saucepan, cook the water and sugar on medium heat, without stirring, until it reaches the boiling point.

3. At the moment when the water-sugar mixture boils, increase the speed on the mixer to high and continue to whip the egg yolks.

4. Continue cooking the water-sugar mixture, without stirring, until it reaches 250°F.

5. At the moment when the sugar syrup reaches 250°F, and with the mixer operating on high speed, remove the sugar syrup from the heat and immediately but slowly pour it into the egg yolks.

6. Continue to whip on high speed for 10 minutes, until the egg-sugar syrup mixture cools to room temperature.

7. Reduce to low speed and pour in the cream. Mix for 1 more minute, until the cream is blended into the egg-sugar syrup mixture and stop the mixer. At this stage, the mixture will be yellow, and have a light, airy texture.

8. Pour the mixture into your ice cream maker and operate according to the manufacturer's instructions until hard.

* *Reaching the right temperature is important in this recipe, so keep a candy thermometer on hand throughout the preparation. You'll need to be precise, but the delicate taste of the final product is worth it!*

Hazelnut Amaretto Ice Cream

Makes 15 balls

1 cup whole milk

1 cup whipping cream

1 vanilla bean, split in half lengthwise

3/4 cup sugar

4 egg yolks

1/2 cup coarsely ground hazelnuts

2 tablespoons amaretto

1. In a saucepan, bring the milk, cream, vanilla bean, and half of the sugar to the scalding point over medium heat.

2. In a bowl, beat the egg yolks and the remaining sugar with a wire whisk until smooth and uniform.

3. When the mixture in the saucepan begins to foam, reduce the heat and quickly stir in the yolk mixture. Remove the vanilla bean and scrape the seeds back into the saucepan.

4. Stirring constantly with a wooden spoon, cook the custard over low heat until it reaches 175°F.

(Continued on page 48)

5. Remove immediately from the heat and continue stirring, so that the custard does not overcook.

6. Pour the custard into a clean bowl through a fine mesh strainer, so that the liquid is smooth and lump-free.

7. While the custard is still warm, add the hazelnuts and amaretto and mix well. It is important to do this while the custard is warm, so that the flavors are fully absorbed.

8. Cover the custard with plastic wrap and let cool slightly, then place in the refrigerator for at least 4 hours, until very cold.

9. Transfer the cold custard to the bowl of your ice cream maker and process according to the manufacturer's instructions.

Chocolate and Chili Ice Cream

(See picture on opposite page)

Makes 15 balls

1 cup whole milk

1 1/2 cups whipping cream

1 vanilla bean, split in half lengthwise

3/4 cup sugar

4 egg yolks

6 ounces bittersweet chocolate, cut into pieces

2 tablespoons crushed dry chili

1. In a saucepan, bring the milk, 1 cup of the cream, vanilla bean, and half of the sugar to the scalding point over medium heat.

2. In a bowl, beat the egg yolks and the remaining sugar with a wire whisk until smooth and uniform.

3. When the mixture in the saucepan begins to foam, reduce the heat and quickly stir in the yolk mixture. Remove the vanilla bean and scrape the seeds back into the saucepan.

4. Using a wooden spoon, stir the custard constantly and cook over low heat until it reaches 175°F.

5. Remove immediately from the heat and continue stirring, so that the custard does not overcook.

6. Pour the custard into a clean bowl through a fine mesh strainer, so that the liquid is smooth and lump-free.

7. Separately, in a small saucepan heat the remaining 1/2 cup of cream over medium heat until it reaches the boiling point. Mix in the chocolate pieces using a wooden spoon, reduce heat, and continue cooking over low heat, mixing constantly, until the chocolate is smooth and glossy.

8. While the custard is still warm, add the chocolate mixture and the chili and mix well. It is important to do this while the custard is warm so that the flavors are fully absorbed.

9. Cover the custard with plastic wrap and let cool slightly, then place in the refrigerator for at least 4 hours, until very cold.

10. Transfer the cold custard to the bowl of your ice cream maker and process according to the manufacturer's instructions.

Vincento Ice Cream

Makes 15 balls

1/2 cup whole milk

1 1/2 cups whipping cream

1 vanilla bean, split in half lengthwise

2/3 cup sugar

4 egg yolks

1/2 cup Vincento or other sweet dessert wine

1. In a saucepan, bring the milk, cream, vanilla bean, and half of the sugar to the scalding point over medium heat.
2. In a bowl, beat the egg yolks and the remaining sugar with a wire whisk until smooth and uniform.
3. When the mixture in the saucepan begins to foam, reduce the heat and quickly stir in the yolk mixture. Remove the vanilla bean and scrape the seeds back into the saucepan.
4. Using a wooden spoon, stir the custard constantly and cook over low heat until it reaches 175°F.
5. Remove immediately from the heat and continue stirring, so that the custard does not overcook.
6. Pour the custard into a clean bowl through a fine mesh strainer, so that the liquid is smooth and lump-free.
7. Add the wine and mix well. It is important to do this while the custard is warm so that the flavor is fully absorbed.
8. Cover the custard with plastic wrap and let cool slightly, then place in the refrigerator for at least 4 hours, until very cold.
9. Transfer the cold custard to the bowl of your ice cream maker and process according to the manufacturer's instructions.

Dried Fruit in Cherry Liqueur Ice Cream

Makes 15 balls

6 ounces dried apricots, dates or figs, finely chopped

2 tablespoons cherry liqueur

1 cup whole milk

1 cup whipping cream

1 vanilla bean, split in half lengthwise

3/4 cup sugar

6 egg yolks

1. Soak the dried fruit in the cherry liqueur for at least 2 hours.
2. In a saucepan, bring the milk, cream, vanilla bean, and half of the sugar to the scalding point over medium heat.
3. In a bowl, beat the egg yolks and the remaining sugar with a wire whisk until smooth and uniform.
4. When the mixture in the saucepan begins to foam, reduce the heat and quickly stir in the yolk mixture. Remove the vanilla bean and scrape the seeds back into the saucepan.
5. Using a wooden spoon, stir the custard constantly and cook over low heat until it reaches 175°F.
6. Remove immediately from the heat and continue stirring, so that the custard does not overcook.
7. Pour the custard into a clean bowl through a fine mesh strainer, so that the liquid is smooth and lump-free.

8. Cover the custard with plastic wrap and let cool slightly, then place in the refrigerator for at least 4 hours, until very cold.

9. Mix the cold custard with the soaked dried fruit, transfer to the bowl of your ice cream maker, and process according to the manufacturer's instructions until hard.

White Chocolate with
Chocolate Liqueur Ice Cream

Makes 15 balls

1 cup whole milk

1 cup whipping cream

1 vanilla bean, split in half lengthwise

3/4 cup sugar

4 egg yolks

5 ounces white chocolate, cut into pieces

2 tablespoons chocolate liqueur

1. In a saucepan, bring the milk, cream, vanilla bean, and half of the sugar to the scalding point over medium heat.

2. In a bowl, beat the egg yolks and the remaining sugar with a wire whisk until smooth and uniform.

3. When the mixture in the saucepan begins to foam, reduce the heat and quickly stir in the yolk mixture. Remove the vanilla bean and scrape the seeds back into the saucepan.

4. Using a wooden spoon, stir the custard constantly and cook over low heat until it reaches 175°F.

5. Remove immediately from the heat and continue stirring, so that the custard does not overcook.

6. Pour the custard into a clean bowl through a fine mesh strainer, so that the liquid is smooth and lump-free.

7. Separately, melt the chocolate in the microwave until it is liquid. Add immediately to the warm custard, and mix well. It is important to do this while the custard is warm and the chocolate is fully melted, so that the flavors are fully absorbed.

8. Cover the custard with plastic wrap and let cool slightly, then place in the refrigerator for at least 4 hours, until very cold.

9. Transfer the cold custard to the bowl of your ice cream maker and process according to the manufacturer's instructions until the ice cream is hard.

10. Open the ice cream maker while it is operating and pour in a few drops of the chocolate liqueur. Wait while the ice cream maker makes 2 turns, then add a few more drops of liqueur. Continue in this manner until all the liqueur has been added. Let the machine operate for 2 more turns, then turn it off.

Marshmallow Ice Cream

(See picture on opposite page)

Makes 15 balls

1 cup whole milk

1 cup whipping cream

1 vanilla bean, split in half lengthwise

3/4 cup sugar

4 egg yolks

6 ounces colored marshmallows, cut into pieces

1. In a saucepan, bring the milk, cream, vanilla bean, and half of the sugar to the scalding point over medium heat.

2. In a bowl, beat the egg yolks and the remaining sugar with a wire whisk until smooth and uniform.

3. When the mixture in the saucepan begins to foam, reduce the heat and quickly stir in the yolk mixture. Remove the vanilla bean and scrape the seeds back into the saucepan.

4. Using a wooden spoon, stir the custard constantly and cook over low heat until it reaches 175°F.

5. Remove immediately from the heat and continue stirring, so that the custard does not overcook.

6. Pour the custard into a clean bowl through a fine mesh strainer, so that the liquid is smooth and lump-free.

7. Cover the custard with plastic wrap and let cool slightly, then place in the refrigerator for at least 4 hours, until very cold.

8. Transfer the cold custard to the bowl of your ice cream maker, add the marshmallow pieces, and process according to the manufacturer's instructions.

Vanilla with Sweet Chili Ice Cream

Makes 15 balls

1 cup whole milk

1 cup whipping cream

1 vanilla bean, split in half lengthwise

3/4 cup sugar

4 egg yolks

1/4 cup sweet chili sauce

1. In a saucepan, bring the milk, cream, vanilla bean, and half of the sugar to the scalding point over medium heat.

2. In a bowl, beat the egg yolks and the remaining sugar with a wire whisk until smooth and uniform.

3. When the mixture in the saucepan begins to foam, reduce the heat and quickly stir in the yolk mixture. Remove the vanilla bean and scrape the seeds back into the saucepan.

4. Using a wooden spoon, stir the custard constantly and cook over low heat until it reaches 175°F.

5. Remove immediately from the heat and continue stirring, so that the custard does not overcook.

6. Pour the custard into a clean bowl through a fine mesh strainer, so that the liquid is smooth and lump-free.

(Continued on page 54)

7. While the custard is still warm, add the chili sauce and mix well. It is important to do this while the custard is warm so that the flavors are fully absorbed.

8. Cover the custard with plastic wrap and let cool slightly, then place in the refrigerator for at least 4 hours, until very cold.

9. Transfer the cold custard to the bowl of your ice cream maker and process according to the manufacturer's instructions.

* *Sweet chili sauce can be found in Asian food stores and specialty shops.*

Lemon Meringue and
Grand Marnier Ice Cream

Makes 15 balls

Meringue Kisses
2 cold egg whites

1/2 cup sugar

2 teaspoons lemon zest

Ice Cream
1 1/2 cups whole milk

1/2 cup whipping cream

1 vanilla bean, split in half lengthwise

2/3 cup sugar

6 egg yolks

2 tablespoons Grand Marnier

1. Preheat the oven to 250°F. Line a baking sheet with parchment paper.

2. In the bowl of a standing mixer, using the whisk attachment, beat the egg whites on high speed until foamy.

3. Gradually add the sugar, and continue beating until stiff peaks form.

4. Using a rubber spatula, fold in the lemon zest until the mixture is smooth and uniform.

5. Using a teaspoon, place 1-inch rounds of the mixture onto the prepared baking sheet, leaving 1/2 inch between each round.

6. Bake for 1 hour. Remove from the oven and place on a wire rack to cool.

7. To prepare the ice cream, place the milk, cream, vanilla bean, and half of the sugar in a saucepan and bring to the scalding point over medium heat.

8. In a bowl, beat the egg yolks and the remaining sugar with a wire whisk until smooth and uniform.

9. When the mixture in the saucepan begins to foam, reduce the heat and quickly stir in the yolk mixture. Remove the vanilla bean and scrape the seeds back into the saucepan.

10. Using a wooden spoon, stir the custard constantly and cook over low heat until it reaches 175°F.

11. Remove immediately from the heat and continue stirring, so that the custard does not overcook.

12. Pour the custard into a clean bowl through a fine mesh strainer, so that the liquid is smooth and lump-free.

13. While the custard is still warm, add the Grand Marnier and mix well. It is important to do this while the custard is warm so that the flavors are fully absorbed.

14. Cover the custard with plastic wrap and let cool slightly, then place in the refrigerator for at least 4 hours, until very cold.

15. Transfer the cold custard to the bowl of your ice cream maker and process according to the manufacturer's instructions until the ice cream is soft.

16. Open the ice cream maker while it is operating and crumble in the meringue kisses. Close the ice cream maker and continue to operate until the ice cream is hard.

Zuppa Inglese Ice Cream

Makes 15 balls

1 cup whole milk

1 cup whipping cream

1 vanilla bean, split in half lengthwise

1 1/4 cups sugar

10 egg yolks

8 ladyfingers, cut into quarters

1/4 cup boiling water

3 tablespoons amaretto

1. In a saucepan, bring the milk, cream, vanilla bean, and 1/2 cup of sugar to the scalding point over medium heat.

2. In a bowl, beat the egg yolks and 1/2 cup of sugar with a wire whisk until smooth and uniform.

3. When the mixture in the saucepan begins to foam, reduce the heat and quickly stir in the yolk mixture. Remove the vanilla bean and scrape the seeds back into the saucepan.

4. Using a wooden spoon, stir the custard constantly and cook over low heat until it reaches 175°F.

5. Remove immediately from the heat and continue stirring, so that the custard does not overcook.

6. Pour the custard into a clean bowl through a fine mesh strainer, so that the liquid is smooth and lump-free.

7. Cover the custard with plastic wrap and let cool slightly, then place in the refrigerator for at least 4 hours, until very cold.

8. Transfer the cold custard to the bowl of your ice cream maker and process according to the manufacturer's instructions until soft.

9. While the ice cream maker is operating, mix together the boiling water and the remaining 1/4 cup of sugar in a bowl. Pour in the amaretto and mix well.

10. Soak the ladyfingers quarters in the amaretto syrup for 30 minutes.

11. When the ice cream is soft, open the ice cream maker while it is operating and pour in the soaked ladyfingers, with any remaining syrup. Close the ice cream maker and continue to operate until the ice cream is hard.

SORBET

Sorbets are light and fruity, made without any eggs, cream or milk. They may be served during multi-course meals in which the courses have different flavors and diverse seasonings. In such cases, a single scoop of sour sorbet between courses is served to neutralize the palate, enabling diners to savor the distinct flavors of each course.

Sorbets are also served as a light dessert after a heavy meal. Two or three small scoops in a tall glass, or a single scoop served in a bowl with fresh fruit, make a simple and elegant dessert. Sorbet is also a surprising and lovely accompaniment to a rich dessert.

Of course, both children and adults will delight in a scoop of sorbet, on a cone or in a cup, on a hot summer's day.

Tips and Techniques

- The base of every sorbet is the syrup. There are many syrup recipes, but the one described below is my favorite. It's easy to make, keeps well, and is an excellent base for all the sorbets in this book.

- I recommend preparing the syrup in advance. This means you won't have to worry about making it on the day you're preparing the sorbet. Prepared syrup can be stored in the refrigerator for up to one month in a sealed container.

- The sugar syrup recipe calls for white sugar and glucose. While the sugar may be replaced with an alternative sweetener, the glucose cannot be replaced. Glucose, in liquid form, can be purchased at specialty baking stores, through catalogues, or online. If you chose to replace the sugar, make sure you use a sweetener that has an equivalent sweetness.

- All of the recipes below require ripe, fresh fruit, unless otherwise stated. The sweetness of the fruit has been taken into account when working out the quantities of each ingredient, so be sure to notice if a recipe says very ripe or almost ripe.

- If you are using frozen fruit, you will probably need to increase the amount of sugar syrup a little. To be sure that your sorbet has just the right amount of sweetness, I recommend tasting the mixture after it has been chilled, and just before pouring it into your ice cream maker. The chilled mixture should be a little sweeter than ripe fruit, and a little sweeter than what you want in your final sorbet, because during the freezing process, some of the sweetness will be lost.

- Adding alcohol to your sorbet is possible and recommended—just choose a schnapps or liqueur that complements the flavors in the sorbet. The perfect ratio is 1 tablespoon of alcohol for every cup of sorbet mixture (syrup + fruit). If you exceed that ratio, you will likely disrupt the freezing point of the mixture, and your sorbet won't freeze properly.

- If you'd like to remove alcohol from a recipe, that's fine too. There is no need to make any alterations to the other ingredients.

- Sorbet can be kept in the freezer for at least two weeks. If you want to freshen up frozen sorbet before serving, defrost it for a few minutes, then pour it into your ice cream maker for one or two spins.

- Sorbet is generally served hard. The exact time it takes to make sorbet varies from ice cream maker to ice cream maker, so please follow the manufacturer's instructions on your machine.

Basic Sugar Syrup

Makes 5 cups

2 cups water

3 cups sugar

1/4 cup glucose

1. In a saucepan, bring the water, sugar, and glucose to the boiling point over medium heat.
2. Remove from the heat and cool to room temperature.
3. Transfer to the refrigerator for at least 1 hour.

FRUITY FAVORITES

Fresh seasonal fruit is the secret to a successful sorbet. Use juicy figs, ripe peaches, and sweet pineapples to make these fresh and refreshing recipes.

Orange Sorbet

(See picture on opposite page)

Makes 10 balls

1 cup sugar syrup (page 57)

1 3/4 cups freshly squeezed orange juice

1 tablespoon Triple Sec or other orange liqueur

1. Mix the sugar syrup, orange juice, and Triple Sec in a bowl and place in the refrigerator for at least 30 minutes.
2. Transfer the chilled mixture to the bowl of your ice cream maker and process according to the manufacturer's instructions.

Nectarine Sorbet

Makes 10 balls

8 large ripe nectarines, peeled, pitted, and coarsely chopped

1 cup sugar syrup (page 57)

1 teaspoon fresh lemon juice

1. In a blender or food processor, purée the nectarines until smooth.
2. Transfer 1 3/4 cups of purée to a bowl. If there is extra purée, freeze for later use.
3. Mix in the sugar syrup and lemon juice and place in the refrigerator for at least 30 minutes.
4. Transfer the chilled mixture to the bowl of your ice cream maker and process according to the manufacturer's instructions.

Green Apple Sorbet

(See picture on opposite page)

Makes 10 balls

6 large Granny Smith apples, cored and coarsely chopped

1 cup sugar syrup (page 57)

1 teaspoon fresh lemon juice

1. In a blender or food processor, purée the apples until smooth.
2. Strain the puréed apples through a fine mesh strainer. Transfer 1 1/2 cups of the purée to a bowl. If there is extra purée, freeze for later use.
3. Mix in the sugar syrup and lemon juice and place in the refrigerator for at least 30 minutes.
4. Transfer the chilled mixture to the bowl of your ice cream maker and process according to the manufacturer's instructions.

Melon Sorbet

Makes 10 balls

1 small ripe sweet melon, peeled, seeded, and coarsely chopped

1 cup sugar syrup (page 57)

1 teaspoon fresh lemon juice

1. In a blender or food processor, purée the melon until smooth.
2. Transfer 1 1/2 cups of purée to a bowl. If there is extra purée, freeze for later use.
3. Mix in the sugar syrup and lemon juice and place in the refrigerator for at least 30 minutes.
4. Transfer the chilled mixture to the bowl of your ice cream maker and process according to the manufacturer's instructions.

Strawberry Sorbet

Makes 10 balls

1 pound fresh strawberries, washed and hulled

1 cup sugar syrup (page 57)

1 teaspoon fresh lemon juice

1. In a blender or food processor, purée the strawberries until smooth.
2. Transfer 1 3/4 cups of purée to a bowl. If there is extra purée, freeze for later use.
3. Mix in the sugar syrup and lemon juice and place in the refrigerator for at least 30 minutes.
4. Transfer the chilled mixture to the bowl of your ice cream maker and process according to the manufacturer's instructions.

Cherry Sorbet

(See picture on opposite page)

Makes 10 balls

1 pound cherries, pitted

1 cup sugar syrup (page 57)

1 teaspoon fresh lemon juice

1. In a blender or food processor, purée the cherries until smooth.
2. Transfer 1 3/4 cups of purée to a bowl. If there is extra purée, freeze for later use.
3. Mix in the sugar syrup and lemon juice and place in the refrigerator for at least 30 minutes.
4. Transfer the chilled mixture to the bowl of your ice cream maker and process according to the manufacturer's instructions.

Guava Sorbet

Makes 10 balls

5 large pink guava, peeled and coarsely chopped

1 cup sugar syrup (page 57)

1 teaspoon fresh lemon juice

1. In a blender or food processor, purée the guava until smooth.
2. Transfer 1 3/4 cups of purée to a bowl. If there is extra purée, freeze for later use.
3. Mix in the sugar syrup and lemon juice and place in the refrigerator for at least 30 minutes.
4. Transfer the chilled mixture to the bowl of your ice cream maker and process according to the manufacturer's instructions.

Peach Sorbet

Makes 10 balls

5 large fresh peaches, pitted and coarsely chopped

1 cup sugar syrup (page 57)

1 tablespoon peach schnapps

1 teaspoon fresh lemon juice

1. In a blender or food processor, purée the peaches until smooth.
2. Transfer 1 3/4 cups of purée to a bowl. If there is extra purée, freeze for later use.
3. Mix in the sugar syrup, peach schnapps, and lemon juice and place in the refrigerator for at least 30 minutes.
4. Transfer the chilled mixture to the bowl of your ice cream maker and process according to the manufacturer's instructions.

Passion Fruit Sorbet

(See picture on opposite page)

Makes 10 balls

1 pound passion fruit

1 cup sugar syrup (page 57)

1 tablespoon Triple Sec or other orange liqueur

1. Scoop out the contents of the passion fruit so that you have 1 1/2 cups and place in a bowl.
2. Mix in the sugar syrup and Triple Sec and place in the refrigerator for at least 30 minutes.
3. Transfer the chilled mixture to the bowl of your ice cream maker and process according to the manufacturer's instructions.

Kiwi Sorbet

Makes 10 balls

10 large ripe kiwi, peeled and coarsely chopped

1 cup sugar syrup (page 57)

1 teaspoon fresh lemon juice

1. In a blender or food processor, purée the kiwi until smooth.
2. Transfer 1 3/4 cups of purée to a bowl. If there is extra purée, freeze for later use.
3. Mix in the sugar syrup and lemon juice and place in the refrigerator for at least 30 minutes.
4. Transfer the chilled mixture to the bowl of your ice cream maker and process according to the manufacturer's instructions.

Apricot Sorbet

Makes 10 balls

14 large, very ripe apricots, peeled, pitted, and coarsely chopped

1 cup sugar syrup (page 57)

1 teaspoon fresh lemon juice

1. In a blender or food processor, purée the apricots until smooth.
2. Transfer 1 3/4 cups of purée to a bowl. If there is extra purée, freeze for later use.
3. Mix in the sugar syrup and lemon juice and place in the refrigerator for at least 30 minutes.
4. Transfer the chilled mixture to the bowl of your ice cream maker and process according to the manufacturer's instructions.

Pineapple Sorbet

(See picture on opposite page)

Makes 10 balls

1 large pineapple, peeled and coarsely chopped

1 cup sugar syrup (page 57)

1 teaspoon fresh lemon juice

1. In a blender or food processor, purée the pineapple until smooth.
2. Transfer 1 3/4 cups of purée to a bowl. If there is extra purée, freeze for later use.
3. Mix in the sugar syrup and lemon juice and place in the refrigerator for at least 30 minutes.
4. Transfer the chilled mixture to the bowl of your ice cream maker and process according to the manufacturer's instructions.

Papaya Sorbet

Makes 10 balls

1 large papaya, peeled, seeded, and coarsely chopped

1 cup sugar syrup (page 57)

1 teaspoon fresh lemon juice

1. In a blender or food processor, purée the papaya until smooth.
2. Transfer 1 3/4 cups of purée to a bowl. If there is extra purée, freeze for later use.
3. Mix in the sugar syrup and lemon juice and place in the refrigerator for at least 30 minutes.
4. Transfer the chilled mixture to the bowl of your ice cream maker and process according to the manufacturer's instructions.

Plum Sorbet

Makes 10 balls

10 large, very ripe red plums, peeled, pitted, and coarsely chopped

1 cup sugar syrup (page 57)

1 teaspoon fresh lemon juice

1. In a blender or food processor, purée the plums until smooth.
2. Transfer 1 3/4 cups of purée to a bowl. If there is extra purée, freeze for later use.
3. Mix in the sugar syrup and lemon juice and place in the refrigerator for at least 30 minutes.
4. Transfer the chilled mixture to the bowl of your ice cream maker and process according to the manufacturer's instructions.

Raspberry Sorbet

(See picture on opposite page)

Makes 10 balls

1 pound fresh raspberries

1 cup sugar syrup (page 57)

1 teaspoon fresh lemon juice

1. In a blender or food processor, purée the raspberries until smooth.
2. Transfer 1 3/4 cups of purée to a bowl. If there is extra purée, freeze for later use.
3. Mix in the sugar syrup and lemon juice and place in the refrigerator for at least 30 minutes.
4. Transfer the chilled mixture to the bowl of your ice cream maker and process according to the manufacturer's instructions.

Blackberry Sorbet

Makes 10 balls

1 pound fresh blackberries

1 cup sugar syrup (page 57)

1 teaspoon fresh lemon juice

1. In a blender or food processor, purée the blackberries until smooth.
2. Transfer 1 3/4 cups of purée to a bowl. If there is extra purée, freeze for later use.
3. Mix in the sugar syrup and lemon juice and place in the refrigerator for at least 30 minutes.
4. Transfer the chilled mixture to the bowl of your ice cream maker and process according to the manufacturer's instructions.

Pomegranate Sorbet

Makes 10 balls

1 cup sugar syrup (page 57)

1 3/4 cups fresh pomegranate juice

1 tablespoon Triple Sec

1. Mix the sugar syrup, pomegranate juice, and Triple Sec in a bowl and place in the refrigerator for at least 30 minutes.
2. Transfer the chilled mixture to the bowl of your ice cream maker and process according to the manufacturer's instructions.

Mango Sorbet

(See picture on opposite page)

Makes 10 balls

3 large, almost ripe mangos, peeled and coarsely chopped

1 cup sugar syrup (page 57)

1 teaspoon fresh lemon juice

1. In a blender or food processor, purée the mangos until smooth.
2. Transfer 1 3/4 cups of purée to a bowl. If there is extra purée, freeze for later use.
3. Mix in the sugar syrup and lemon juice and place in the refrigerator for at least 30 minutes.
4. Transfer the chilled mixture to the bowl of your ice cream maker and process according to the manufacturer's instructions.

Pink Fig Sorbet

Makes 10 balls

10 large ripe juicy pink figs, coarsely chopped

1 cup sugar syrup (page 57)

1 teaspoon fresh lemon juice

1. In a blender or food processor, purée the figs until smooth.
2. Transfer 1 3/4 cups of purée to a bowl. If there is extra purée, freeze for later use.
3. Mix in the sugar syrup and lemon juice and place in the refrigerator for at least 30 minutes.
4. Transfer the chilled mixture to the bowl of your ice cream maker and process according to the manufacturer's instructions.

WITH A TWIST

With a variety of unusual flavor combinations, the sorbets in this section create truly unique taste sensations.

Red Grapefruit and Campari Sorbet

(See picture on opposite page)

Makes 10 balls

1 cup sugar syrup (page 57)

1 1/2 cups freshly squeezed red grapefruit juice

2 tablespoons Campari

1. Mix the sugar syrup, grapefruit juice, and Campari in a bowl and place in the refrigerator for at least 30 minutes.
2. Transfer the chilled mixture to the bowl of your ice cream maker and process according to the manufacturer's instructions.

Pear and Calvados Sorbet

Makes 10 balls

7 large ripe pears, peeled, cored, and coarsely chopped

1 cup sugar syrup (page 57)

2 tablespoons Calvados

1 teaspoon fresh lemon juice

1. In a blender or food processor, purée the pears until smooth.
2. Transfer 1 3/4 cups of purée to a bowl. If there is extra purée, freeze for later use.
3. Mix in the sugar syrup, Calvados, and lemon juice and place in the refrigerator for at least 30 minutes.
4. Transfer the chilled mixture to the bowl of your ice cream maker and process according to the manufacturer's instructions.

Cherry Tomato Sorbet

(See picture on opposite page)

Makes 10 balls

2 cups ripe cherry tomatoes

1/2 cup sugar

3/4 cup sugar syrup (page 57)

1 teaspoon fresh lemon juice

1. In a saucepan, place the tomatoes and the sugar and cook over medium heat until the mixture reaches the boiling point.
2. When the mixture boils, reduce the heat to low and continue to cook for 30 minutes, stirring occasionally.
3. Remove the mixture from the heat and transfer to a food processor or blender. Add the sugar syrup and blend.
4. Pour the mixture through a medium strainer into a bowl. Stir in the lemon juice and place in the refrigerator for at least 30 minutes.
5. Transfer the chilled mixture to the bowl of your ice cream maker and process according to the manufacturer's instructions.

Wild Berry and Grappa Sorbet

Makes 10 balls

1 pound fresh wild berries

1 cup sugar syrup (page 57)

1 tablespoon grappa

1 teaspoon fresh lemon juice

1. In a blender or food processor, purée the berries until smooth.
2. Transfer 1 3/4 cups of purée to a bowl. If there is extra purée, freeze for later use.
3. Mix in the sugar syrup, grappa, and lemon juice and place in the refrigerator for at least 30 minutes.
4. Transfer the chilled mixture to the bowl of your ice cream maker and process according to the manufacturer's instructions.

Tequila Margarita Sorbet

(See picture on opposite page)

Makes 8 balls

1 cup sugar syrup (page 57)

1 cup fresh lemon juice

3 tablespoons gold tequila

1 teaspoon finely minced lemon zest

1. Mix the sugar syrup, lemon juice, tequila, and lemon zest in a bowl and place in the refrigerator for at least 30 minutes.
2. Transfer the chilled mixture to the bowl of your ice cream maker and process according to the manufacturer's instructions.

Rosemary Sorbet

Makes 8 balls

2 cups sugar syrup (page 57)

1 stem fresh rosemary

3 tablespoons fresh lemon juice

1. In a small saucepan, mix together 1 cup of sugar syrup with the rosemary and cook until it reaches the boiling point.
2. Remove from heat and pour through a fine mesh strainer into a bowl. Add the remaining cup of sugar syrup and mix well.
3. Add the lemon juice and mix well. Place in the refrigerator for at least 1 hour.
4. Transfer the chilled mixture to the bowl of your ice cream maker and process according to the manufacturer's instructions.

Limoncello Sorbet

(See picture on opposite page)

Makes 8 balls

1 cup sugar syrup (page 57)

1 cup fresh lemon juice

2 tablespoons limoncello

1. Mix the sugar syrup, lemon juice, and limoncello in a bowl and place in the refrigerator for at least 30 minutes.
2. Transfer the chilled mixture to the bowl of your ice cream maker and process according to the manufacturer's instructions.

* *Served with fresh fruit salad and a light sauce of passion fruit juice and confectioners' sugar, this sorbet makes a refreshing finish to a spicy meal.*

FROZEN DESSERTS

In this chapter, you'll find a selection of mouthwatering desserts in which ice cream is either the main ingredient or a perfect accompaniment.

Most of the recipes suggest certain flavors of ice cream or sorbet, but feel free to experiment with your own favorite flavor combinations. There are countless variations to each recipe, and something to suit every occasion. Whether you're planning a casual afternoon brunch or a gourmet feast for special guests, a festive family meal or a romantic dinner for two, I'm sure one of the recipes below will make an appropriate (and delicious) dessert. Of course, you can also prepare one of these frozen desserts for yourself, as an indulgent snack on a quiet evening at home.

Tips and Techniques

- Before starting any recipe, read through the whole recipe in advance, and prepare all of your ingredients. This will make following the recipe much easier.

- Many of the recipes require ice cream to be poured into molds or spread over cakes. For these recipes, remove the ice cream from the ice cream maker while the texture is soft, so it is easy to pour and spread. If you are using homemade ice cream that has already been frozen or store-bought ice cream, let the ice cream defrost for about 15 minutes in the refrigerator before using.

- There are plenty of opportunities to be creative in these recipes, so let your imagination—and your taste buds—lead the way. Use the recipes as guides, and alter the ingredients according to your favorite flavors, or what's in season. You can also be creative in the presentation, by serving the desserts in distinct glasses or colorful bowls, and topping with rich syrups or other garnishes. Remember—ice cream is fun, so have fun preparing it!

- A number of recipes call for frozen pop molds. These can be bought at most houseware stores and online. In the summertime, they can also be found at many supermarkets.

- It has been my experience that frozen pops must be placed in the freezer for at least 24 hours before serving. Although it can be hard to wait this long (especially for children), the fun of eating a well-frozen pop is worth it!

FAVORITES

Fun and festive, these classic ice cream desserts will bring smiles to the faces of every ice cream lover you know.

Banana Split

(See picture on opposite page)

Serves 2

1/3 cup sugar

3 large ripe bananas

1/4 cup butter

1 ball French Vanilla Ice Cream (page 10)

1. In a non-stick fry pan, cook the sugar over low heat until it is a light caramel color.

2. Place the bananas in the pan and fry until golden brown on each side.

3. When the bananas are ready, use a slotted spoon or spatula to transfer them to a deep serving plate.

4. Return the pan to the heat and add the butter. Continue to cook, while stirring with a wooden spoon, until the butter is brown and syrupy.

5. Place the ice cream on the bananas, pour over the syrup, and serve immediately.

Baked Alaska

(See picture on opposite page)

Makes 8

8 balls Chocolate Brandy Ice Cream (page 44)

3 egg whites

1/2 cup sugar

1. Preheat oven to broil (500°F or higher).
2. Scoop 8 balls of chocolate ice cream onto a tray and place in the freezer until well frozen.
3. In the bowl of an electric mixer, using the whisk attachment, beat the egg whites on high speed until soft and foamy.
4. Gradually add the sugar while the mixer is operating, and continue to beat until the mixture forms stiff peaks and has a glossy texture.
5. On a baking dish or oven-proof tray, arrange the balls of ice cream. Using a disposable pastry bag, pipe the meringue around each ball, so that the balls are completely covered with the meringue.
6. Broil the meringue-covered balls for 1 or 2 minutes, until the meringue is golden brown. Remove from the oven and serve immediately.

Fried Ice Cream

Serves 10

10 balls ice cream, your choice of flavor

1/2 cup all-purpose flour

1/3 cup cornstarch

2 tablespoons baking powder

1 egg

3/4 cup cold water

Vegetable oil, for frying

Chocolate, caramel, or maple syrup for garnish

1. Scoop 10 balls of ice cream onto a tray and place in the freezer until well frozen.
2. Put the flour, cornstarch, and baking powder in a bowl and mix well with a wire whisk.
3. Separately, mix the egg with the water in a small bowl.
4. Gradually add the egg-water mixture to the flour-cornstarch mixture until it is smooth and lump-free.
5. Heat at least 1 inch of oil in a deep pan or deep fryer.
6. When the oil reaches 375°F, remove the balls of ice cream from the freezer. One at a time, dip each ice cream ball into the egg-flour mixture, making sure that the ice cream is fully coated in the batter.
7. Use a large spoon to transfer the coated ice cream balls to the hot oil, and fry until the batter is golden.
8. Transfer to a serving plate, garnish as desired, and serve immediately.

Ice Cream in Espresso

(See picture on opposite page)

Serves 8

**8 balls Italian Vanilla Ice Cream
(page 13)**

8 servings fresh espresso

8 teaspoons Frangelico or Tia Maria

1. In advance, prepare individual cups and saucers that can hold one scoop of ice cream and be placed in the freezer.
2. Just before serving, fill each cup with a scoop of ice cream and place in the freezer.
3. While the ice cream is in the freezer, prepare the espresso in an espresso machine or stovetop espresso maker.
4. When the espresso is ready, remove the cups of ice cream from the freezer and pour a single serving of espresso over each one. Pour a teaspoon of Frangelico over each scoop of ice cream and serve immediately.

Nutty Pops

Makes 8

**1 recipe Hazelnut Amaretto Ice Cream,
soft (page 46)**

1 cup chopped walnuts

1. Prepare the ice cream according to the recipe, removing it from the ice cream maker while soft. If you are using ice cream that is already frozen, place it in the refrigerator for about 15 minutes to soften.
2. Pour the soft ice cream into the frozen pop molds, filling each mold to the top. Quickly press in the pop sticks and place the molds in the freezer. Make sure the pops are standing vertically, and freeze for at least 24 hours.
3. Just before serving, spread the walnuts evenly onto a large plate.
4. Remove the frozen pops from the freezer and, one at a time, carefully remove each frozen pop from its mold. Gently press the pop into the walnuts, rolling it slowly so that it is completely covered in walnuts. Lay the pop gently on a dish and repeat with the other pops.
5. At this stage, the pops may be served immediately, or returned to the freezer for serving later.

Belgian Waffles

(See picture on opposite page)

Makes 4

1 cup whole milk

1/4 cup sugar

4 eggs

1/2 teaspoon salt

Dash of vanilla extract

3/4 cup all-purpose flour

1/2 cup melted butter

Butter, for waffle iron

Thinly sliced pineapple, for garnish

8 balls Italian Vanilla Ice Cream (page 13)

Caramel sauce, for garnish

1. In the bowl of an electric mixer, beat the milk, sugar, eggs, salt, and vanilla extract on low speed. Gradually add half of the flour while the mixer is operating, and continue to mix for 3 minutes.

2. While the mixer is still operating, add the butter and the rest of the flour. Mix until the dough is smooth and oily.

3. Transfer the dough to a clean bowl and cover with plastic wrap. Place in the refrigerator for 30 minutes.

4. Remove the dough from the refrigerator and divide into 4 equal parts. Roll each part into a ball. In the meantime, lightly grease a waffle iron with butter and heat.

5. When the waffle iron is hot, place one of the balls of dough into the iron and close the lid.

6. Cook until the waffle is golden brown. Remove from the iron and set aside. Repeat until all of the waffles have been cooked.

7. Top each waffle with a thin slice of pineapple, a scoop of vanilla ice cream and a spoonful of caramel sauce.

* *Belgian waffles can be topped with any combination of ice cream and toppings you like. Try serving with Espresso Ice Cream and fresh strawberries, Mint Ice Cream with chocolate sauce, or Peanut Butter Ice Cream and honey.*

Chocolate Almond Pops

(See picture on opposite page)

Makes 8

1 recipe Chocolate Brandy Ice Cream, soft (page 44)

4 ounces bittersweet chocolate, cut into pieces

1 cup chopped roasted almonds

1. Prepare the ice cream according to the recipe, removing it from the ice cream maker while soft. If you are using ice cream that is already frozen, place it in the refrigerator for about 15 minutes to soften.

2. Pour the soft ice cream into the frozen pop molds, filling each mold to the top. Quickly press in the pop sticks and place the molds in the freezer. Make sure the molds are standing vertically, and freeze for at least 24 hours.

3. Just before serving, melt the chocolate in a double boiler.

4. At the same time, spread the almonds evenly onto a large plate.

5. Remove the frozen pops from the freezer and, one at a time, carefully remove each frozen pop from its mold. Use a small ladle to pour some melted chocolate onto the pop and allow it to cool for a few seconds. Gently press the chocolate-covered pop into the almonds, rolling it slowly so that it is completely covered in almonds. Lay the pop gently on a dish and repeat with the other pops.

6. At this stage, the pop may be served immediately, or returned to the freezer, for serving later.

CAKES

There's nothing quite like a homemade ice cream cake to celebrate birthdays, graduations, and every other special occasion.

Tricolatte Cake

(See picture on opposite page)

Serves 10

Cake Batter

4 eggs, separated

2/3 cup sugar

1/2 cup all-purpose flour

3 tablespoons confectioners' sugar

1 recipe Chocolate Brandy Ice Cream (page 44)

1 recipe Espresso Ice Cream (page 20)

1 recipe French Vanilla Ice Cream (page 10)

1. Preheat the oven to 375°F. Line a baking sheet with parchment paper.

2. In the bowl of an electric mixer, using the whisk attachment, beat the egg whites on high speed until soft and foamy.

3. Gradually add half of the sugar, and continue to beat until stiff peaks form.

4. Transfer the egg whites to a larger bowl and place the egg yolks in the emptied bowl of the electric mixer. There is no need to rinse the bowl at this stage.

5. Using the whisk attachment, beat together the egg yolks and the remaining sugar until thick and fluffy.

6. Transfer the egg yolks to the bowl with the egg whites.

7. Sift about 1/3 of the flour over the egg yolks and fold in using a rubber spatula.

8. Fold in the rest of the flour with the rubber spatula, folding until the mixture is smooth and uniform.

9. Using a long palette knife, spread a 1/4-inch layer of batter on the baking sheet.

10. Sprinkle the confectioners' sugar over the batter and bake for 12 minutes, or until golden brown.

11. Remove the cake from the oven and place, with the parchment paper, on a wire rack to cool for 1 hour.

12. About 15 minutes before you are ready to begin assembling the cake, transfer the chocolate ice cream from the freezer to the refrigerator, to soften.

13. When the cake has cooled, turn it over and carefully remove the parchment paper. Place the cake on a work surface, with the side that touched the parchment paper facing up.

14. Place the ring of a 10-inch round springform pan on the cake and,

(Continued on page 94)

using a sharp knife, cut out a circle of cake by tracing the inside of the rim. Save the trimmed pieces of cake for Step 16.

15. Assemble the springform pan and carefully place the circle of cake inside the pan. Pour the soft chocolate ice cream over the cake, and place in the freezer for 15 minutes. Transfer the espresso ice cream to the refrigerator, to soften.

16. Remove the cake from the freezer and arrange the trimmed pieces of cake on the layer of chocolate ice cream.

17. Pour over the espresso ice cream and return to the freezer for 15 minutes. Transfer the vanilla ice cream to the refrigerator, to soften.

18. Remove the cake from the freezer and pour on a layer of vanilla ice cream. Use a long palette knife to level the top of the ice cream. Return to the freezer for at least another 15 minutes, or until ready to serve. Gently remove the sides of the pan before serving.

Florida Cake

(See picture on opposite page)

Serves 10

Cake Batter
4 eggs, separated

2/3 cup sugar

1/2 cup all-purpose flour

3 tablespoons confectioners' sugar

1 recipe Honey and Spice Ice Cream (page 36)

1 recipe Kumquat Ice Cream (page 40)

1/2 recipe Orange Sorbet (page 58)

1. Preheat the oven to 375°F. Line a baking sheet with parchment paper.

2. In the bowl of an electric mixer, using the whisk attachment, beat the egg whites on high speed until soft and foamy.

3. Gradually add half of the sugar, and continue beating until stiff peaks form.

4. Transfer the egg whites to a larger bowl and place the egg yolks in the emptied bowl of the electric mixer. There is no need to rinse the bowl at this stage.

5. Using the whisk attachment, beat together the egg yolks and remaining sugar until thick and fluffy.

6. Transfer the egg yolks to the bowl with the egg whites.

7. Sift about 1/3 of the flour over the egg yolks and fold in using a rubber spatula.

8. Fold in the rest of the flour with the rubber spatula, folding until the mixture is smooth and uniform.

9. Using a long palette knife, spread a 1/4-inch layer of batter on the baking sheet.

10. Sprinkle the confectioners' sugar over the batter and bake for 12 minutes, or until golden brown.

(Continued on page 96)

11. Remove the cake from the oven and place, with the parchment paper, on a wire rack to cool for 1 hour.

12. About 15 minutes before you are ready to begin assembling the cake, transfer the honey ice cream from the freezer to the refrigerator, to soften.

13. When the cake has cooled, turn it over and carefully remove the parchment paper. Place the cake on a work surface, with the side that touched the parchment paper facing up.

14. Place the ring of a 10-inch round springform pan on the cake and, using a sharp knife, cut out a circle of cake by tracing the inside of the rim. Save the trimmed pieces of cake for Step 16.

15. Assemble the springform pan and carefully place the circle of cake inside the pan. Pour the soft honey ice cream over the cake, and place in the freezer for 15 minutes. Transfer the kumquat ice cream to the refrigerator, to soften.

16. Remove the cake from the freezer and arrange the trimmed pieces of cake on the layer of honey ice cream.

17. Pour over the kumquat ice cream and level using a long palette knife. Return to the freezer for 15 minutes and transfer the orange sorbet to the refrigerator, to soften.

18. Remove the cake from the freezer and pour on a layer of orange sorbet. Use a long palette knife to level the top of the sorbet. Return to the freezer for at least another 15 minutes, or until ready to serve. Gently remove the sides of the pan before serving.

Buenos Aires Cake

(See picture on opposite page)

Serves 10

Cake Batter
4 eggs, separated

2/3 cup sugar

1/2 cup all-purpose flour

3 tablespoons confectioners' sugar

1 recipe Nougat Ice Cream (page 45)

1 recipe Dulce de Leche Ice Cream (page 16)

1. Preheat the oven to 375°F. Grease a 10-inch round springform pan.

2. In the bowl of an electric mixer, using the whisk attachment, beat the egg whites on high speed until soft and foamy.

3. Gradually add half of the sugar and continue beating until stiff peaks form.

4. Transfer the egg whites to a larger bowl and place the egg yolks in the emptied bowl of the electric mixer. There is no need to rinse the bowl at this stage.

5. Using the whisk attachment, beat together the egg yolks and remaining sugar until thick and fluffy.

(Continued on page 98)

6. Transfer the egg yolks to the bowl with the egg whites.

7. Sift about 1/3 of the flour over the egg yolks and fold in using a rubber spatula.

8. Fold in the rest of the flour and the confectioners' sugar with the rubber spatula, and continue to fold until the mixture is smooth and uniform.

9. Pour the batter into the springform pan and bake for 25 minutes, or until golden brown.

10. When baked, transfer to a wire cooling rack and cool for 1 hour.

11. About 15 minutes before you are ready to begin assembling the cake, transfer the nougat ice cream from the freezer to the refrigerator, to soften.

12. When the cake has cooled, run a knife along the inside edge of the pan to loosen the cake. Gently remove the sides of the pan and turn out the cake onto a work surface, so that the bottom of the pan is facing up.

13. Using a serrated knife, cut the cake crosswise into 2 equal layers. Place your hand on the bottom of the pan and, using the serrated knife, separate the bottom of the pan from the upper layer of the cake.

14. Set aside both cake layers and reassemble the springform pan.

15. Put one of the cake layers back into the pan. Pour the soft nougat ice cream on top and level with a long palette knife. Put the second cake layer on top of the ice cream and place in the freezer for 15 minutes. Transfer the dulce de leche ice cream to the refrigerator, to soften.

16. Remove the cake from the freezer and pour the soft dulce de leche ice cream on top. Level using a long palette knife, then return to the freezer for at least 15 minutes, or until ready to serve.

17. Just before serving, take out of the freezer and gently remove the sides of the pan.

Roulade

Serves 8

4 eggs, separated

2/3 cup sugar

1/2 cup all-purpose flour

3 tablespoons confectioners' sugar

1 recipe ice cream, your choice of flavor, soft

1. Preheat the oven to 375°F. Line a baking sheet with parchment paper.

2. In the bowl of an electric mixer, using the whisk attachment, beat the egg whites on high speed until soft and foamy.

3. Gradually add half of the sugar and continue to beat until stiff peaks form.

4. Transfer the egg whites to a larger bowl and place the egg yolks in the emptied bowl of the electric mixer. There is no need to rinse the bowl at this stage.

5. Using the whisk attachment, beat together the egg yolks and remaining sugar until thick and fluffy.

6. Transfer the egg yolks to the bowl with the egg whites.

7. Sift about 1/3 of the flour over the egg yolks and fold in using a rubber spatula.

8. Fold in the rest of the flour with the rubber spatula, folding until the mixture is smooth and uniform.

9. Using a long palette knife, spread a 1/4-inch layer of batter on the baking sheet.

10. Sprinkle the confectioners' sugar over the batter and bake for 12 minutes, or until golden brown.

11. Remove the cake from the oven and place, with the parchment paper, on a wire rack to cool for 1 hour.

12. When the cake is cool, turn it over and carefully remove the parchment paper. Place the cake on a work surface, with the side that touched the parchment paper facing up.

13. Using a long palette knife, spread the soft ice cream on the surface of the cake, then roll it up into a roulade.

14. Place the roulade in the freezer for at least 1 hour. Remove from the freezer just before serving, cut into 1-inch slices, and serve.

* *To make a chocolatey dessert, dip each slice in melted chocolate before serving.*

Raspberry Charlotte

(See picture on opposite page)

Serves 10

Cake Batter
4 eggs, separated

2/3 cup sugar

1/2 cup all-purpose flour

3 tablespoons confectioners' sugar

2 recipes Raspberry Ice Cream (page 28)

1 quart fresh raspberries

1. Preheat the oven to 375ºF. Line a 16 by 14-inch baking sheet with parchment paper.

2. In the bowl of an electric mixer, using the whisk attachment, beat the egg whites on high speed until soft and foamy.

3. Gradually add half of the sugar, and continue to beat until stiff peaks form.

4. Transfer the egg whites to a larger bowl and place the egg yolks in the emptied bowl of the electric mixer. There is no need to rinse the bowl at this stage.

5. Using the whisk attachment, beat together the egg yolks and remaining sugar until thick and fluffy.

6. Transfer the egg yolks to the bowl with the egg whites.

7. Sift about 1/3 of the flour over the egg yolks and fold in using a rubber spatula until uniform.

8. Fold in the rest of the flour with the rubber spatula, folding until the mixture is smooth and uniform.

9. Transfer the batter to a disposable pastry bag and pipe 3-inch strips perpendicular to the long edge of the baking sheet. There should be no spaces between the strips, and they should run from the top to the bottom of the sheet. Repeat along the other long edge of the baking sheet, to make two 3 by 16-inch strips of batter.

10. Sprinkle the confectioners' sugar over the batter and bake for 12 minutes, or until golden brown.

11. Remove the cakes from the oven and place, with the parchment paper, on a wire rack to cool for 1 hour.

12. About 15 minutes before you are ready to assemble the cake, transfer the ice cream to the refrigerator to soften.

13. When the cakes are cool, turn them over and carefully remove the parchment paper.

14. Press one of the cakes along the inside rim of a 10-inch springform pan, so that the side that touched the parchment paper is facing inwards. In the same manner, press in the other cake to form a continuous crust around the pan.

15. Pour in the soft ice cream and level using a palette knife. Place the cake in the freezer for at least 30 minutes, or until ready to serve.

16. Just before serving, remove the cake from the freezer and arrange the raspberries on top. Gently remove the sides of the pan and serve.

ELEGANT ENDINGS

These distinctive desserts are perfect finales to any fine meal.

Marsala Soaked Pears with Ice Cream

(See picture on opposite page)

Makes 12

6 large, almost ripe pears, peeled, cored, and halved lengthwise

1/2 bottle Marsala wine

1 recipe Italian Vanilla Ice Cream (page 13)

1. Lay the pear halves in a wide pan and pour over the wine. Cook over medium heat until the wine reaches the boiling point.

2. Reduce the heat and continue cooking until you can easily pierce the pears with a fork.

3. Transfer the pears to a bowl using a slotted spoon, and set aside to cool to room temperature.

4. Return the pan with the wine to the heat and continue cooking until the wine reduces to a syrup.

5. Pour the syrup into a deep serving dish. Arrange the pears inside the serving dish, so that the cut side of each pear is facing up. Place a small scoop of ice cream on each pear, and serve immediately.

Dried Apple and Prune Soup with Ice Cream

Serves 4

1/2 cup dried apples

1/2 cup pitted prunes

1/2 cup sugar

1 cup water

1/2 teaspoon cinnamon

1 tablespoon prune liqueur

4 balls Italian Vanilla Ice Cream (page 13)

1. In a saucepan, place the dried apples, prunes, sugar, water, and cinnamon and cook over medium heat until it reaches the boiling point.

2. When the mixture boils, reduce the heat and continue to cook on low heat for 20 minutes, until it has a syrupy texture.

3. Remove the mixture from the heat and mix in the liqueur until well blended. Set aside to cool to room temperature.

4. Place in the refrigerator for at least 4 hours. The mixture may be stored in a sealed container in the refrigerator for up to four days.

5. To serve, pour a ladle of the mixture into a soup bowl and top with a scoop of vanilla ice cream.

Cassata

(See picture on opposite page)

Serves 8

1 recipe Italian Vanilla Ice Cream, soft (page 13)

1/2 cup diced candied fruit

1 tablespoon Marsala wine

4 ounces bittersweet chocolate, cut into pieces

1. Line the inside of an 8-inch round bowl with plastic wrap, so that a wide margin of plastic wrap extends from the rim.

2. In a separate bowl, place the ice cream, candied fruit, and wine and mix well.

3. Transfer the ice cream mixture to the lined bowl. Draw together the edges of plastic wrap and pinch, so that the ice cream is sealed. Place in the freezer for at least 4 hours.

4. About 40 minutes before serving, melt the chocolate in a double boiler until liquid.

5. Remove the bowl of ice cream from the freezer and unwrap the top. Turn the bowl upside and place on the serving dish. Remove the bowl and the plastic wrap from the ice cream, to reveal a dome of speckled ice cream.

6. Quickly and evenly, pour the melted chocolate over the ice cream, so that the whole dome is covered in a thin layer of chocolate.

7. Return to the freezer for another 30 minutes, then slice and serve.

Sorbet in a Fillo Basket

Serves 6

6 10-inch sheets fillo dough, thawed

1/2 cup melted butter

12 balls sorbet, variety of flavors

1. Preheat oven to 400°F. Line a baking sheet with parchment paper.

2. Place 1 sheet of fillo on a work surface. Brush on some melted butter, then place another sheet on top. Brush on more melted butter, then place another sheet of fillo. Repeat until all 6 pieces of fillo are neatly stacked.

3. Use a sharp knife to round the edges of the fillo, so that you have a large circular shape.

4. Place an ovenproof serving bowl upside down on the baking sheet.

5. Lay the stack of fillo pastry on top of the serving bowl, so that the fillo is centered over the bowl. Place a second ovenproof serving bowl on top of the fillo.

6. Bake for 12 minutes, or until golden brown. Remove from the oven and set aside, leaving the serving bowls on either side of the fillo. Allow to cool for 40 minutes.

7. After the fillo has cooled, remove the top bowl to reveal a crispy baked bowl of fillo pastry.

8. Just before serving, fill the fillo bowl with the sorbet and serve.

Chocolate Pavlova and Vanilla Ice Cream

(See picture on opposite page)

Makes 6

3 egg whites

3/4 cup sugar

2 tablespoons cocoa

1/4 cup chopped bittersweet chocolate

1/2 recipe French Vanilla Ice Cream (page 10)

1. Preheat the oven to 350°F. Line a baking sheet with parchment paper.
2. In the bowl of an electric mixer, using the whisk attachment, beat the egg whites on high speed until soft and foamy.
3. Gradually add the sugar while the mixer is operating. Beat until it forms stiff peaks and has a glossy texture.
4. Using a rubber spatula, fold in the cocoa and chocolate.
5. Place a tablespoon of batter onto the baking sheet and, using the back of the spoon, spread the batter to create a 4-inch circle. Repeat with the rest of the batter, leaving 1/2-inch between each circle.
6. Bake for 30 minutes, or until the Pavlovas are firm around the edges. Remove from the oven and place on a wire rack to cool for 30 minutes.
7. To serve, place each Pavlova on an individual serving dish. Top with a small scoop of ice cream and serve immediately.

Roasted Peaches in Amaretto with Almond Ice Cream

Makes 6

6 ripe yellow-flesh peaches, pitted and halved lengthwise

2 tablespoons amaretto

1/4 cup sugar

4 ounces butter, room temperature

1/4 cup water

1 recipe Candied Almond Ice Cream (page 27)

1. Heat a grill pan over high heat. When the pan is hot, place the peach halves inside, so that the cut sides of the peaches touch the pan.
2. Roast the peaches for several minutes, until grill lines appear on the sides touching the pan.
3. Transfer the peaches to a bowl and, while they are still very hot, pour over 1 tablespoon of amaretto. Stir gently.
4. Separately, place the sugar and butter in a small saucepan and cook over medium heat until caramelized and golden.
5. Add the water and the remaining tablespoon of amaretto and cook for 2 to 3 minutes, without stirring, until the sauce is smooth and uniform.
6. Using a slotted spoon, transfer the peaches to a serving tray, arranging them so that the roasted sides face up.
7. Pour the remaining syrup from the peaches into the saucepan with the caramel-amaretto sauce and mix well.
8. Just before serving, place a small scoop of ice cream on each peach half. Pour the caramel sauce over top and serve immediately.

Profiteroles

Makes 20

Profiteroles
1/4 cup water

1/4 cup milk

1/4 cup butter

1 teaspoon sugar

Pinch of salt

1/2 cup all-purpose flour

2 eggs

1 egg, beaten

1 recipe French Vanilla Ice Cream (page 10)

Chocolate Sauce
1 cup whipping cream

5 ounces bittersweet chocolate, cut into pieces

1 teaspoon chocolate liqueur

1. In a small saucepan, over medium heat, bring the water, milk, butter, sugar, and salt to the boiling point.

2. Add the flour and continue to cook while mixing, until the dough comes away from the sides of the saucepan and forms a ball.

3. Transfer the dough to a bowl and mix with a spoon to cool slightly.

4. Add the eggs one at a time, mixing thoroughly after each addition to make sure that the egg is completely incorporated into the dough.

5. Place the dough in the refrigerator for 30 minutes. In the meantime, preheat the oven to 400°F and line a baking sheet with parchment paper.

6. Remove the chilled dough from the refrigerator and, using a teaspoon dipped in lukewarm water, drop spoonfuls of dough onto the baking sheet, 1/2 inch apart. Dip the spoon in the water between each spoonful of dough, and repeat until all of the dough has been placed onto the sheet.

7. Brush each profiterole with the beaten egg and bake for 15 minutes, or until golden brown.

8. Remove from the oven and place on a wire rack to cool for 1 hour.

9. Using a small sharp knife, cut the top off of each profiterole. Fill each profiterole with a spoonful of ice cream, and place in the freezer for 15 minutes, or until the ice cream is well frozen.

10. Just before serving, prepare the chocolate sauce by heating the whipping cream and chocolate pieces in a small saucepan over low heat. When the mixture reaches the boiling point, remove from the heat, add the chocolate liqueur, and stir well.

11. Remove the frozen profiteroles from the freezer and arrange on a serving plate. Pour over the chocolate sauce and serve immediately.

Limoncello Sorbet and Fruit Salad in Tuile Bowls

Serves 8

3 egg whites

3/4 cup confectioners' sugar

2/3 cup all-purpose flour

1/3 cup butter, room temperature

Fruit salad to serve 8

8 balls Limoncello Sorbet (page 78)

1. Preheat oven to 400ºF. Line 2 baking sheets with parchment paper.
2. In the bowl of an electric mixer, place the egg whites, sugar, flour, and butter, and mix on low speed until smooth.
3. Place a heaping tablespoon of batter on one of the baking sheets and, using the back of the spoon, spread the batter to create a 5-inch circle. Repeat to make a total of 8 circles, leaving about 1 inch between each circle.
4. Bake for 9 minutes, or until golden brown.
5. In the meantime, place 16 heat-resistant disposable cups upside down on a work surface.
6. Remove the baked tuiles from the oven and, using a long palette knife, quickly and carefully remove the tuiles, one at a time, from the baking sheet and place on the base of a cup. Place another cup on top of the tuile. Repeat until all 8 tuiles have been sandwiched between 2 disposable cups.
7. Set the tuiles aside for about 10 minutes, until they have cooled, then carefully remove each one from its makeshift mold.
8. Just before serving, place the tuile cups right side up on a serving tray. Fill each with fruit salad, top with a scoop of sorbet, and serve.

* *The tuile bowls take on the shape of the cups you use for molding, so try to find cups that have a wide base.*

Index